THE *Best* OF
WILL
WILLIMON

THE *Best* OF
WILL WILLIMON

Acting Up
in Jesus' Name

Abingdon Press
Nashville

THE BEST OF WILL WILLIMON
ACTING UP IN JESUS' NAME

Copyright © 2000, 2002, 2005, 2006, 2008, 2009, 2010, 2011, 2012 by Abingdon Press

This book is printed on acid-free paper.

Library of Congress Cataloging-in-Publication Data has been requested.

ISBN 978-1-4267-4202-6

12 13 14 15 16 17 18 19 20 21—10 9 8 7 6 5 4 3 2 1

MANUFACTURED IN THE UNITED STATES OF AMERICA

CONTENTS

PREFACE

Will Willimon likes to tell about the time he met with the parents of a young woman who, having heard one of his sermons, had decided to abandon her preparation for a lucrative career and instead volunteer for service in a Third World country. Confronted by the parents' angry questions about what he had said that would lead to such a decision, Willimon replied meekly, "I was just . . . preaching."

His answer to the irate couple notwithstanding, Bishop Willimon rarely "just" does anything. He has carved out a reputation as an outstanding preacher, teacher, teller of stories, and leader of his church. And yet probably more people have encountered Will Willimon in his capacity as a writer than anything else. Over a writing career that spans decades, he has charmed and enlightened everyone from fresh-faced confirmation class graduates to prickly academics. He has lifted up the essential humor of Scripture; teased, cajoled, and wooed a church too accommodated to culture; maintained the high calling of pastors while insisting that ministry belongs to all the baptized; wrestled with the likes of Barth and Wesley; tuned our ears to the echoes of Christian faith in literature and film; argued with anyone who wants to limit God's saving work to those "in the club"; and throughout pointed unerringly to the Cross and Resurrection of Jesus Christ.

This book represents an attempt to capture the best of Will Willimon's writings in a single volume. Whether you've been a Willimon fan for years, or this is your first exposure to this "peculiar prophet," we suggest that you hold on to your seat. It's going to be an invigorating and inspiring—if at times bumpy—ride.

—*the editors*

CHAPTER ONE

JESUS

Though Jesus did not, at first, impress us as the Messiah (by refusing to live up to our expectations of what a messiah is), eventually, some got the point and worshiped him. They adored him, not necessarily as the means to a better world, not as an effective catalyst for social change, but rather as the way God really is, all the way down. He is reality, and in him, we see that reality is peace. True, it is a peace "that passes all understanding." It is not peace that one achieves by studying the course of world history or by meditating upon the human condition. His peace comes as a gift from the one who is known, paradoxically, as the Prince of Peace, the clue to what's really going on in the world, the revelation of who God really is.

So Jesus hangs upon a bloody cross, humiliated before the whole world. The mob taunts, "If you are really tight with God, command your legions of angels to take charge, to come down and defeat your enemies and deliver you."

But Jesus just hanged there. He breathed his last, and he died. This is the way God's kingdom comes? This is the way God wins victory? A stupendous claim, not made before or since by any religion: God not only takes the side of the innocent victim of violence and injustice but becomes one of them.

Jesus advocated no systematic program of human reform, never recommended any collective social adjustments, no matter how badly needed or enlightened. Jesus was not big on ethical codes, had no ideology, did no interesting work in political science or social ethics, and never put forth a plan of action, other than the (seemingly) wildly impractical notions that the first will be last, that we must turn the other cheek to those who strike us, and that we should become like little children.

Likewise, Jesus appears to have had no interest in one of the world's great, abiding illusions—justice. At various times, Jesus was dragged before the agents of justice—Caiaphas (the high priest), the Sanhedrin, Pontius Pilate (Jesus made little distinction between religious power brokers and secular ones). One of the most noble systems of justice ever devised responded to Jesus by torturing him to death. Worldly attempts at justice always involve the strong imposing their wills upon the weak. In crying for justice, the weak are usually demanding power to work their wills upon the strong. Perhaps that's why, in world history, Jesus is usually on the losing side. After the world's revolutions, it's often difficult to tell the vanquished from the victors, morally speaking. People in power tend to act the same, despite why they got there. All of which explains why Jesus never got along well with potentates, religious or otherwise.

Having spoken to his heavenly father, "Father, forgive them, they don't know what they are doing," Jesus now speaks to a criminal. He bypasses us and turns to the thief. He, who was forever instructing his followers, he who was always in prayer to his Father, now converses with a crook—in the disarmingly present tense. Now He, who got into much trouble with us righteous ones because he dared to eat and drink with sinners, now talks and dies with sinners. As Jesus hung in agony upon the cross, there was no one beside him but a thief. Well, not so much a "thief" as probably a "troublemaker," a "rabble-rouser," perhaps an "insurrectionist," maybe more accurately, a "terrorist."

And the criminal said to him, "Jesus, remember me when you come into your kingdom." The wretched man was surely thinking of tomorrow. For there, today with Jesus on a cross and a howling mob in front of him, in horrible agony from the worst form of punishment ever devised by wicked humanity, mocked before the world, any "kingdom" promised by Jesus must be in some distant future.

Jesus surprised him. "Today you will be with me in Paradise" (Luke 23:43). *Today*. What was conceived only as future became present in this promise of Jesus. You might have expected Jesus to say, "Someday, after I'm gone, when God finally gets things together and sets things right, when this horrible miscarriage of justice has been rectified, then you will be with me in my promised kingdom. Just wait until tomorrow."

No, Jesus said, "today you will be with me in Paradise." What a promise to speak to such a person in such horrible hell of crucifixion. Today, paradise.

Now one could say, "today you will be with me in Paradise" because Jesus and the thief were about to die, so that very evening they would be in the paradise of the afterlife. Both Jesus and the thief were on their way to death and therefore on their way to whatever life happens after death. It sure didn't look like paradise from where they were hanging. But I don't think that gets at the shock of what Jesus says here.

I believe that if Jesus had been walking along some Galilean road in the bright sunshine, rather than hanging here on the cross before a darkening sky, and if Jesus and the thief had had many years of life on this earth still ahead of them, I believe that this conversation would have gone exactly the same way.

For when Jesus speaks of "Paradise," he is not talking so much of a place where they may go someday, as *a relationship that they entered today*.

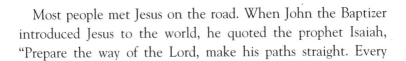

Most people met Jesus on the road. When John the Baptizer introduced Jesus to the world, he quoted the prophet Isaiah, "Prepare the way of the Lord, make his paths straight. Every valley shall be filled, and every mountain and hill shall be made low…and all flesh shall see the salvation of God." In Jesus, God worked a highway construction project, making a road straight through the desert to enslaved humanity. Just as in the exodus, when God made a "way" out of Egyptian slavery to the Promised Land, so Jesus is the "way" to God. How ironic that while we clamored up to God through our intellect, our morality, our architecture, our art, and our institutions (both secular and religious), in Jesus Christ, God slipped in among us. The first name for the church was simply "The Way," not only our way to God but rather God's way to us.

All the gospels present Jesus on a continual road trip—God in motion, urgently making a way to us in defeat of the desert in which we wander. *Euthys*, the Greek word for "immediately" occurs forty-two times in Mark's Gospel. No sooner does Jesus do something than "immediately" he hits the road to elsewhere. Some of Jesus' best words were spoken on the run. Many have wanted to know more about the early childhood and adolescence of Jesus. Matthew and Luke tell us a little about the circumstances of Jesus' birth, and Luke has one story about his going to the Temple in Jerusalem when he was twelve. In Mark, probably the earliest of the gospels, Jesus just shows up out of nowhere, gets baptized by John, and then the Spirit shoos him out into the wilderness. It is as if the gospels want to say that the action only really gets going when Jesus hits the road.

Jesus cannot be explained simply as the next chapter in the long, gradual, forward advance of humanity; his birth to a virgin named Mary signifies that Jesus is present as the miraculous gift of a gracious God, the God-given goal of all human history. The gospels tell us that knowing where this gift came from, who his people were, isn't going to help us much. If you want to know about Jesus, if you want to know him, you've got to meet him on the road.

Sorry if you prefer your God to be with you as a remarkably effective moral teacher or wise sage. In Jesus, humanity and divinity meet. A domesticated Jesus, whose strange, inexplicable mix of humanity and divinity has somehow been made simpler— either human or divine, one or the other, and hence easier for us to understand and to handle—is no Jesus at all. Intellectual humility is required, a willingness to let God be complicatedly incarnate, close to us, rather than the simpler God we thought up on our own. Sometimes the strange, rational impossibility just happens to be true—God was in Christ, reconciling the world to himself.

Sorry if you prefer your God to come at you in an exclusively spiritual, inflated, pale blue and fuzzy vagueness, hermetically sealed from where you actually live. In Jesus, divinity and humanity embrace.

Sometimes people ask, "Can I really trust the Bible, seeing that it is a thoroughly human product, full of all the errors and contradictions that characterize any human endeavor?" The implication is that if Scripture has any human taint, shows any creaturely weakness, the Bible can't be trusted to talk about God. But what if Jesus is true? What if we don't know anything for sure about God, except that which is shown to us by the God-and-human Jesus? What if Jesus really is fully human and fully divine? Then where on earth would we expect to know anything about God, except through a medium that is human? God came to us as we are, met us where we live, in the human words of Scripture that become the very voice of God, in the man Jesus who becomes the very presence of God.

⋙〰⋙〰⋙〰⋙〰⋙

Once there was One who came to us, who touched the untouchables, turned his back upon the world's bright baubles, loved even unto death, and never turned his eyes away from God.

And we hated him for it. He came to us with wide-open hands in gracious invitation, seeking us, both patient with us and hotly pursuing us. And thereby he brought out the very worst in us.

We figured that things between us and God were not all that bad, but when he spoke to us of God, and ourselves, and rubbed our noses in the filthy rags of our presumed righteousness, well, we thought we were good until we met him. He called upon us to attempt great moral feats, then watched as we fell flat on our faces. He invited us to join up with his Kingdom, then set that Kingdom's demands so high that when it came time for us to stand up and show what we were made of, we fled, slithering into the darkness. He said, "Come to me. Take on my yoke." And we with one voice cried, "Crucify him!"

<hr />

Is this Jesus at his most offensive, in his talk of preemptive forgiveness? Is this why we nailed him to the cross, in his forgiving us even before we asked and, what is more, asking us to forgive others? In a sermon on forgiveness, Augustine (Sermon 49.8) said that sometimes people in his church omitted the phrase from the Lord's Prayer that says, "and forgive us our debts as we forgive our debtors." Just passed right over that phrase silently because they knew it would be lying for them to say that aloud. They knew, says Augustine, that they were making a kind of covenant with God in this "forgive us our sins as we forgive the sins of others." In some of the earliest versions of Luke's Gospel, these words are omitted from the Lord's Prayer. Forgiveness is hard.

A rabbi once said to me that, while he admired most of what Jesus said and did, as a Jew, he found these first words from the cross among the most offensive, lamentable, and reprehensible. Why?

"We've had enough Jews crucified by gentiles. We don't need any more Jews forgiving gentiles for killing Jews."

I could see his point. When in my former congregation, a woman, being abused by her boyfriend, said to me, "I've prayed to God for the strength to be able to forgive him," I said to her, "No. First you tell him that he is wrong, that if he abuses you again, you are going to call the cops, have him thrown in jail, and then, and only then, if he stops, then we'll talk forgiveness."

With Jesus, on the cross, the sequence was different. First, he prayed to God to forgive. If we are meant to listen and to learn from the words of Jesus on the cross, this must be among the most distinctive, difficult lessons to learn, this first one.

"Who is this who forgives sin?" his critics asked. This day we, his would-be followers ask, "Who is this who *first* forgives sins—even before anybody has acknowledged the sin?"

"Lord, will you at this time restore the kingdom to Israel?" Jesus' disciples asked after his resurrection. That is, "Lord, will you at this time finally act like a Messiah, mount your war horse, raise a royal army, rout our Roman occupiers, and set up Israel as the nation we are meant to be?"

Christ meant "Messiah," which means the Anointed, the king, the political/military hero. Politics is power, our only means of transcending the problems of this world. "Jesus, when are you at last going to move from spiritual blather to something important—like politics?" Jesus responded by telling his followers that it was not for them to know the times for such things. Jesus seems somewhat evasive, reluctant to come right out and say, "I'm the Messiah you have been expecting," probably because he knew that their messianic expectations were not for someone like him.

At this point, honesty compels me to say that, if you are one of those people with great love for the government or reverent respect for the military that props up government, you will find Jesus a jolt to your sensibilities. The modern state—with its flags, pronouncements, parades, propaganda, public works projects, and assorted patriotic paraphernalia—does not mesh well with Jesus. Patriotism, while perhaps a virtue, has never been regarded as a specifically Christian virtue.

In truth, Jesus was very "political," but not as we expected. After his arrest—by functionaries of the state—Jesus stood before Pontius Pilate, who was seated upon the judgment seat to render a verdict on Jesus.

"So, are you king?" asked Pilate, sarcasm dripping from his urbane Roman lips. Jesus responded, "You have said so," implying that much of this concern about royalty and authority was Pilate's preoccupation, not his. Then Jesus pronounced, "My kingdom is not of this world," or at least, that's how his words are sometimes translated. Closer to the Greek: "My kingdom is not from here." It's a mistake to interpret Jesus as having said, "My kingdom is out of this world, something otherworldly, spiritual even." Rather, Jesus is saying, "My kingdom is not from here, here with all these royal trappings and raw power, here propped up with swords and acting as if it were from God. My reign is not secured by the swords of Caesar's finest. My authority derives from elsewhere."

⊸⫟⊷ ⊸⫟⊷ ⊸⫟⊷ ⊸⫟⊷ ⊸⫟⊷

The Gospels, and indeed all of Scripture, were born in a culture in which people passed information along orally, were careful to repeat things often, told only what was important, and looked for help from eyewitnesses to verify accuracy. The writers of the gospels collected the stories about Jesus that had been circulated orally and wove them into careful and distinctive accounts of what he said and did—and why that matters. Generations of Christians have found these writings to truly reveal God in singular and life-changing ways. Besides, we're justified in giving particular weight to the testimony of those who paid for their friendship with Jesus by their blood.

But Jesus is more than his words remembered; he is interesting not only because of what he said but for who he is. We should therefore also talk about Jesus through the medium of his friends. Paul (whose writings are older than the gospels) never met Jesus until the risen Christ accosted him on the Damascus Road. Yet Paul may know as much about Jesus as those who walked next to him down the Jerusalem Road. Paul seems neither to know nor to care about most of the teachings of Jesus or details of his life before the cross and resurrection, yet Paul's wildly adventurous life after meeting Jesus shows that Paul really knows Jesus. We are right to trust descriptions of Jesus given by those most disrupted by Jesus. Some people around Jesus looked at him and wanted to follow him, pattern their lives after his, and tell everybody about him. The majority of people who met Jesus apparently thought he was nuts and wanted him dead. Sometimes, the burning sun is best viewed by watching those upon whom it shines.

You and I tell stories in order to figure out what sort of world we've got. Stories are fiction that is meant to uncover the deep, real truth about the world. Nobody can live without a story that makes sense of the world and gives us a beginning, a middle, and an end to what could otherwise be a really random world.

And yet, Jesus' parables tend not to explain. They just begin, as if out of nowhere, without context, often in the middle. They are, at times, exasperatingly devoid of important details. As we have noted, few of the parables have well-wrought conclusions. They seem more intent on confusion than clarification. Surely, Jesus could have found a more effective mode of explaining his message—unless explaining of his message was not his chief goal.

Jesus' first hearers share our frustration. "Why do you talk in parables?" his disciples asked. Why, Jesus? Matthew remembers Jesus replying: "To you has been given the gift to understand the great secrets of the kingdom of heaven, even though few of you are the brightest candles in the box. But to the rest of them everything's a riddle. I tell these stories so they can hear things they wouldn't otherwise hear."

First insight: understanding of Jesus, faith in Jesus, the ability to figure out what he's talking about and what he's up to, is a gift of God. It's God's revelation, not some personal intellectual achievement, "I throw out so many of these parables because, listening, they don't hear and, looking, they don't see," says Jesus.

Second insight: mere understanding of Jesus may not be the point. Parables take you deeper. They are a complex, deep way of thinking about the world. It is possible to think too quickly or superficially that you know Jesus. Then, you can pigeonhole Jesus and forget about him, thinking about Jesus in about the same way you think about everything else. You walk away murmuring, "I got it." Maybe the parables want to expose you to the adventure that comes with, "Jesus got me." Maybe Jesus tells these stories in order to make you a character in the story, in order to put your life in the grand narrative of God's salvation of the world.

By the way, just in case you are too pleased with Matthew's explanation of Jesus' penchant for parables, Mark remembers Jesus saying, "Why do I speak in parables? I talk like this so that they won't hear no matter how closely they listen and they won't see no matter how sincerely they look." Why on earth would the church include two passages, from the mouth of Jesus, contradicting one another? It's a riddle.

Are you willing to follow a Savior who deals in incomprehensible riddles and crazy jokes?

Third insight: eventually, this sometimes contradictory, conflicted quality of Scripture, which often is so exasperating may, with time, become beloved. Sometimes, Jesus reaches out for us; sometimes, Jesus pushes away. Jesus is God with us, not God controlled, explained, and tamed by us. Jesus not only spoke in parables; Jesus is a parable.

There was a time when people thought that Jesus told lots of these stories because he was attempting to put difficult ideas into simple, everyday rural idiom. You can readily see that explanation doesn't do justice to the complex, disarming, disorienting quality of most of these parables. Their surprise endings, or lack of endings, their cryptic, enigmatic quality, the way they delight in making heroes out of scalawags and Samaritans suggest that parables are meant to dislodge more than to explain.

Why, Jesus? Why do you talk in riddles? Story by story, Jesus is moving us from the safe, secure world we thought we knew to another world where all is strange and things don't turn out as expected, and something's afoot. You are forced to review your inherited assessment of the world. You are disconnected from your old, familiar world so that, now, you might be connected to a whole new world. God turns out to be other than you previously had assumed. The kingdom of God dawns in that moment when, from the ditch, you look down the Jericho Road, having lost your last, best hope of rescue by a nice savior, only to see coming toward you the lousy Samaritan you despise.

⸙ ⸙ ⸙ ⸙ ⸙

There were times when Jesus went alone into the desert to pray, but we know next to nothing about what actually transpired in that solitude. More typical is for Jesus to be constantly interacting with people—mixing it up with a crowd, meeting travelers on the road, and most typical of all, eating and drinking with gusto at parties. In a world where women were relegated to the home, Jesus welcomed them to travel with him on the road from Galilee to Jerusalem and was entertained by them in their homes. He seemed intent on making the private go public. He loved the give-and-take of public debate.

As a supremely social, communal person, whatever it was that Jesus felt called by his heavenly Father to do, he had no interest in doing it by himself. His life implies that we are fully human, not in our solitude or loneliness but only through a web of relationships and connections with others, including God. Today, Christian worship is generally known not for the opportunities it offers for hushed serenity but rather for its very noisy communitarian conviviality. The chief Christian liturgical act (the Eucharist or Lord's Supper) occurs at a dinner table. Jesus' own gregarious life made oxymoronic the term "solitary Christian." You can't do this faith solo.

When asked to cite the single most important of the commandments, Jesus flatly refused and instead offered a two-fold command to love God with everything we've got *and* to love "your neighbor as yourself," as if one made no sense bereft of the other.

Whining critics complained, "The disciples of John the Baptist fast often and go about with long faces," (we can tell they're religious; they look so miserable) "but your disciples are always at parties, and eating and drinking." Jesus retorted, "When the groom shows up, do the wedding guests look sad? It's party time!" It's hard to imagine a similar complaint against Jesus' contemporary disciples.

God in Jesus Christ is encountered not through solitary walks in the woods, or even by reading a book (!), but rather at a mundane dinner table, doing that most utterly carnal of acts—sharing food and drink with friends. Jesus really was God incarnate—God localized, humane, and available in the flesh. Thus, Jesus opened his Sermon on the Mount with, "Blessed are those who hunger and thirst for righteousness, for they shall be filled." Nobody goes away hungry from a banquet. Presumably, Jesus' message has more traction among the hungry and thirsty than among the fat and happy. If you are filled, pleased with current arrangements, there's little Jesus can do for you. Don't you find it fascinating that Jesus pitched his message more to those who could say, "I want more. I'm still hungry," than to those who said, "No thanks, I'm full"?

CHAPTER TWO

TRINITY

In order to keep God distant and vague (and *irrelevant*) many people want to keep God simple, uncomplicated, and abstract. These are the dear folk who say, "Well, I'm not sure that I'm very religious, but I do believe in God. After all, isn't that what it's all about?"

The problem is that once we discovered that God was in Christ, things got complicated not because the church wanted to make the simple faith of Jesus complex and confusing but because we discovered in Jesus that God was at once much more demanding and much more interesting than we had first thought. In Christ, God was reiterated in ways that meant we were forced to expand our notions of God. We could have gotten along quite nicely without the Trinity had John the Baptist not intruded into our settled arrangements with God by shouting, "Here is the Lamb of God who takes away the sin of the world!" (John 1:29). Once Jesus showed up—one "conceived by the Holy Spirit," born of a poor peasant woman in Judea, God in the flesh, teaching, working wonders among us in the "power of the Spirit," suffering and dying at our hands, rising after three days, returning to the very people who crucified him, breathing his Holy Spirit upon us—well, we had to talk about God in a way that only complex, dynamic trinitarian theology could do justice. After being met by Jesus, we could never again think of God in the simple, uncomplicated way as we had before.

The Holy Spirit contemporizes, reveals, and imparts our redemption here and now. Sadly for us preachers, the Holy Spirit seems to be the most neglected person of the Trinity in contemporary theology. We preachers need a robust conviction of the Holy Spirit's work because we, unlike most academic interpreters of the Christian faith or of Scripture, must stand up and speak a word to God's people, here, now. The Holy Spirit is the power of God, empowering humanity to know God. The Holy Spirit is God's agency in preaching, that which makes a sermon work.

The Holy Spirit is not some impersonal force, not some vague sense, but rather has a distinct personality, as portrayed in Scripture. I would characterize that personality as dynamic, difficult, destructive, life-giving, creative but disruptively creative (Genesis 1; Acts 2). In the power of the Holy Spirit Jesus told us to pray for the coming of God's reign and to not lose heart (Matt 6:10). But not because God was holding something back. It was now but not yet. It is not fully here, not only because a nonviolent God refuses to force or to coerce that reign upon us. (We may still turn away and reject, refuse, and decline.) Yet the Kingdom also seemed distant, even as Jesus stood beside us, because it was *Jesus* who stood beside us. The nearness of the Kingdom, in Jesus, gave us a close look into what God's kingdom was really like. Jesus made us pray, "Thy Kingdom come, thy will be done on earth as it is in heaven," now, here as it will be then, there.

Confidence in the power of the Holy Spirit to overcome all of our self-imposed resistance, to construct true Christians out of the stuff of us sinners, makes the work of the Holy Spirit the engine that drives all Wesleyan theology. The Holy Spirit is not exotic, optional equipment for a Christian. We depend on the Holy Spirit as much as we depend on air. In fact, John Wesley spoke of "spiritual respiration" to emphasize the necessity of being constantly connected to the Holy Spirit. (See Sermon 45, "The New Birth," §II.4.) Like air filling our lungs, the spirit of God fills our lives, making us refreshed and ready to do God's work. Stop breathing God and our spiritual lives wilt. Because our spiritual respiration is not involuntary, unlike our natural breathing, we must concentrate on being receptive to the Holy Spirit through prayer and the sacraments, Bible study, and other spiritual practices that assist us in cultivating life in the Spirit.

It is the nature of the Holy Spirit to work through a multitude of means to make God present to us, to give us not only the presence of God to us but also the power of God working in us.

Thus I met two older women who have begun and sustained a ministry within one of our local jails for youthful offenders. They visit twice a week and volunteer to teach literacy courses to the inmates. They also make sure that every young man's birthday is celebrated with a cake and presents provided by local United Methodist churches.

"I have really surprised myself," said one of the women. "I've always been a rather shy person, not the type to venture out and attempt new things. Can you believe what God has done for these young men through someone like me?"

It was, for me, a wonderfully Wesleyan testimonial to the effects of the Holy Spirit. I guess the wild story in Acts 2 is true.

God's got this thing for us. God is determined—through Creation, the sagas of the Patriarchs, the words of the prophets, the teaching of the law, and the birth and death of the Christ—to get close, very close, too close for comfort, in fact. Sorry, if you thought when we said "God" we had in mind an impersonal power, a fair-minded, balanced bureaucrat who is skilled in the dispassionate administration of natural law from a safe distance in eternity. Our God is intensely, unreservedly personal. The God of Israel and the church refuses to be an abstraction or a generality. In the Bible, God gets angry, repents, threatens, promises, punishes, takes back, and resumes the conversation. Only persons do such things and, when we do them, it is a sign of our personal worth, the highest of our personhood, our passionate valuing of something over nothing, not of our grubby anthropocentric imperfection.

The most important decision in Christian theology is to decide whether you will speak of God as a person or as a concept, as a name or as an idea. Talk about God as, to use Paul Tillich's term, "ultimate reality," and you will get a safe, dead abstraction that you can utilize in whatever salvation project you happen now to be working. Name God as Father, Son, and Holy Spirit, and God will enlist you in God's move upon the world. That's one of the things we mean when we say that "Jesus is Lord" or "Jesus is God's only Son." This God is shockingly personal, available, and present. It's also what we mean when we say that "Jesus is Savior." This is in no way detraction from the Father's immense deity. There are gods who could not risk getting close. We are killers who tend to resent our would-be saviors. Anybody who would love me risks great pain because of me. So most "gods" are careful to keep their distance through abstraction and idealization. "Gods" are, by definition, distant, high, and lifted up.

The one whom Israel calls Yahweh and the church knows as Trinity is so great as to be utterly personal, available, and richly present to us. This God is against detached reserve. "God never rests," says Luther, constantly pursuing, presenting to us. You can't get much closer to us, to the real us, than a cross.

Christians are witnesses to a great cosmic incursion, an invasion in which God, rather than being distant from the world, has daringly entered the world (Gal 4:4). The world is God's contested territory in a vast program of reclamation.

⊸⬗⊶ ⊸⬗⊶ ⊸⬗⊶ ⊸⬗⊶ ⊸⬗⊶

But now, midway through Friday, look. The One whom Jesus calls "Father" is not in heaven, sitting on a throne, preparing to swoop down sometime and fix everything. The Father is there with the Son, hanging on a cross, now in intimate conversation with the Son, therefore not as the Son. We don't want to overhear such terrible, terrifying words, "My God, why have you abandoned me," because we don't want to know that that's the kind of God we've got, the kind of God who does not always work the world to our benefit, the kind of God who, when it gets dark, doesn't immediately switch on the lights but rather comes and hangs out with us, on the cross, in the dark, and lets us in on the most intimate of conversations within the very heart of the Trinity.

The Father is one with the Son, in the power of the Holy Spirit. Yet the Father, in infinite love, has sent the Son out to the far country to us sinners. Away from the Father in order to be close to those who have abandoned the Father, the Son risks separation from the Father, risks not only abandonment but also dismemberment from his true identity. The Son comes very close to us, so close that he bears our sinfulness, bears the brunt of our viciousness. And the Father, who is complete righteousness and holiness, cannot embrace the sin that the Son so recklessly, lovingly bears, so the Father must abandon the Son on the cross because the Father is both love and righteousness. Here, in this word from the cross, is the unthinkable: a separation, because of love, in the heart of the fully loving, inseparable Trinity. In this world, love is the cause of some of life's greatest tragedies, and we know that there is no way completely to love anyone without the risk of pain because of that love. Sure, it's an inadequate human analogy, but we grope in our talk of such a mystery. What a

The Best of Will Willimon

sacrifice the Father is making in the Son's sacrifice, in the sacrificial power of the Spirit. There is a real division in the heart of the Trinity at this moment on the cross, and because the Trinity is inherently indivisible, the magnitude of the sacrifice is massive. The division that is part of the pain that must be borne by a God who would come out, in both righteousness and love, to save us.

━━━━ ━━━━ ━━━━ ━━━━ ━━━━

What is God like? Jesus replies: a homeowner sleeps, secure in his ownership (Luke 12:39). During the night, he awakes in horror; a thief has broken into his home and ripped off everything. He dearly wishes that he had known that the time of his dormancy would be the time of a robbery, but he didn't. Now he's the loser. Jesus warns that each of us should live as if we were about to get ripped off by God. Losers, wake up!

I'll grant that Jesus' parable is not the most flattering image of God. God's a thief who breaks in and rips you off?

Jesus, teller of this outrageous tale, incarnates the thief who shatters the illusion of time's normalcy. Jesus strides in and takes time. What's "new" in Jesus is the "now" of Jesus. Others had talked "kingdom of God." (Luke, for instance, tirelessly reiterates that Jesus Christ is not new: Christ is the fulfillment of the ancient promises of God to Israel.) It took Jesus to preach that the "kingdom of God *has come near*" (Luke 10:9). What was new is that Jesus said that the day of the Lord is *now*. He met our apocalyptic expectation with his earth-shaking presence. Trouble is, once apocalyptic expectation became messianic reality—present—we discovered that this was not at all the presence we thought we were awaiting. We looked at Jesus and said, "Please, not so near, not so excruciatingly present, not in this place, not in this Jew. Not in any Jew, in fact."

"The Kingdom of God has come near" is ambiguous news. Jesus discovered that in the congregational reaction to his first

18

sermon in Nazareth (Luke 4). Things went OK as he read the poetic words of Isaiah. Then Jesus had the gall to announce, "*Today* these past words are now (fulfilled) in your hearing," and church was out. It was the nearness, the "nowness" that caused crisis and demanded change, now. Salvation is always easier when it is delayed, future and therefore harmless. Here, now is a demanding gift. In a threatening tone of voice Paul preached, "Now is the day of salvation" (2 Cor 6:2).

Yet here's the paradox. It was not only that Jesus was God present, here, now. It was also that God was in *Jesus Christ* reconciling the world to himself (2 Cor 5:19). In Jesus, we met the God whom we had not known, did not want to know. God *pro nobis*, for us, tends always to be perceived as the God *anti nobis*, the God against us. God is hidden precisely in God's availability to the world. In Jesus "incarnation" was not only in flesh but also in time. And when our time is commandeered by *that* particular God, well, we get nervous and our defenses against God are activated. Some of us wanted to see God but were disappointed that God was in Jesus of Nazareth, now, here.

Most people in our society appear to want God to be generic, abstract, vague, distant, and arcane. "God? Oh, can't say anything too definite about God. God is large and indistinct." For many of us God is this big, blurry concept that we can make to mean about anything we like, something spiritual, someone (if we have any distinct notions about God) whom we can make over so that God looks strikingly like us.

> Ruin'd nature now restore, Now in mystic union join Thine to ours, and ours to thine.

In Jesus of Nazareth, God got physical, explicit, and peculiar, and God came close—too close for comfort for many. Jesus Christ is God in action, God refusing to remain a general idea or a high-sounding principle. Jesus Christ is God in motion toward us, God refusing to stay enclosed in God's own divinity. Many people think of God as a vaguely benevolent being—who never actually gets around to *doing* anything.

It is as if we are threatened by the possibility that God might truly be an active, intervening God who shows up where we live. We've designed this modern world, controlled by us, functioning rather nicely on its own, thank you, everything clicking along in accord with natural laws, served on command by technological wonders of our creation. So who needs a God who relishes actually showing up and doing something? We modern people are loath to conceive of a God who is beyond our control or a world other than the one that is here solely for our personal benefit.

This is the deistic God of the philosophers, a minimalist, inactive, unobtrusive, noninvasive, detached God who is just about as much of a God as we moderns can take. There's a reason why many thoughtful modern people seem so determined to sever Jesus from the Trinity, to render Jesus into a wonderful moral teacher who was a really nice person, someone who enjoyed lilies and was kind to children and people with disabilities. To point to a peripatetic Jew from Nazareth who wouldn't stay confined within our boundaries for God and say, "Jesus is not only a human being but also God," well, it's just too unnerving for us enlightened modern people to handle. Note how frequently many people refer to "God" and how seldom they refer to "Christ," and you will know why the statement "in Christ God was reconciling the world to himself" (2 Cor.5:19) is a threatening disruption to many people's idea of a God who stays put.

At Pentecost we gathered, Jews from every nation on earth, to remember the gift of the first five books of the Bible to Israel (thus the name for the festival, *penta*= "five"; see Acts 2). No sooner had we gathered to look back in memory than there was the sound "like the rush of a violent wind" that came "suddenly from heaven," and we found our foundations shaken, disrupted, and the Holy Spirit descending, moving us forward. Everybody began to testify to what God was doing in our midst; everybody heard one another speak in spite of our national differences. We had gathered to remember the past, only to have the Holy Spirit thrust us into a new, unexpected future.

This is rather typical behavior for the Holy Spirit, the third person of the Trinity. Just as the Spirit (the "wind from God") brooded over the waters at Creation, bringing forth life where there had been little but darkness and death (Gen. 1:2), so the Holy Spirit descended at Pentecost bringing forth a new people, the church. The Holy Spirit appears to love to create, to initiate, and to bring something new out of something old, to give possibility and potentiality in times and places where it was thought that we had reached a dead end. Creation, empowerment, speaking and hearing, and yes, even disruption of our placid present with lively, unexpected future—all are typical deeds of the Holy Spirit.

Thus the same Spirit who hovered over the dark waters at Creation got the story of Jesus started by descending upon Jesus at his baptism "like a dove," saying, "You are my Son, the Beloved; with you I am well pleased" (Mark 1:10-11). (Interestingly, when Matthew told of Jesus' baptism, Matthew implied that the "Spirit of God" descended "like a dove and [alighted] on him" and the voice "from heaven" addressed everyone standing there [Matt. 3:16-17].) It is of the nature of the Holy Spirit to reveal, to speak to us intimately, personally in the depths of our hearts, and to address us publicly, principally through preaching. Thus whenever we read Scripture in our worship, it is typical to pray a Prayer for Illumination that calls upon God to "open our hearts and minds by the power of your Holy

Spirit so that as the word is read and proclaimed we may hear what you have to say to us today."

Because the Holy Spirit is a member of the Trinity, that is, God, the Holy Spirit enables us truly to encounter Christ in our reading of Scripture. The Holy Spirit produces Scripture, enlightens our reading and hearing of Scripture, and enables us to perform Scripture. Miraculously, when we read Scripture, Christ stands among us, present through our reading and hearing of mere words.

The Holy Spirit tells Christians what to think about God and how to speak to and for God. Paul said that though we don't always know just how to pray, the Holy Spirit helps us. Jesus told his disciples that when they haul you into a courtroom (note that he didn't say *if* they arrest you and throw you in the slammer but *when* they arrest you), don't plan your defense speeches to the court in advance: "When they bring you before the synagogues, the rulers, and the authorities, do not worry about how you are to defend yourselves or what you are to say; for the Holy Spirit will teach you at that very hour what you ought to say" (Luke 12:11-12). That's why, when Scripture is read or a sermon is preached, we often pray, "Lord, open our hearts and minds by the power of your Holy Spirit so that we can hear what you want to say to us today," or words to that effect. The Holy Spirit is a great teacher, telling us things we could never come up with on our own. Just as Jesus preached in "the power of the Spirit" in Nazareth (Luke 4:14), so Jesus' Holy Spirit enables us to speak about Jesus and to hear Jesus. Even faith in Jesus is a gift of Jesus in the power of the Spirit. As Paul put it, "No one can say 'Jesus is Lord' except by the Holy Spirit" (1 Cor. 12:3).

There is a kind of effusiveness about God, an effervescent, overflowing quality.

Augustine spoke of this in a passage in his great book *The City of God*. Augustine spoke of the "plentitude" of God. As evidence of this, Augustine mentioned the effusiveness whereby God created all of the flowers in the world. We might have stopped creating flowers after one or two beautiful specimens. But God didn't stop. God kept creating multitudes of flowers, all in different shapes and colors and kinds. Not only are they beautiful, Augustine notes, but see the glory in how they will turn their heads toward the sun, bending toward the light. We might have been content, as humans, with just a few flowers and their splendor. God didn't stop with a few, because God is effusive, overflowing with love and creativity. God is ubiquitous, plenitudinous.

I feel sorry for Fundamentalist Christians, who earnestly attempt to reduce this effusive, overflowing God to five or six "fundamentals." It is tough to get this God down to a list of five or six of anything, because our God is effusive.

I sorrow for the self-described "Progressive Christian" scholar who recently dumbed things down to "the essence of Christianity"—five or six vague platitudes that allegedly sum up Jesus. This isn't progress but regress to a "god" who is considerably more flat and dull than the Trinity.

So, as Christians, we don't have one Gospel, we have four. Four Gospels! One might have thought that we could have stopped with one, saying to ourselves, "Matthew fairly well got it right, let's all go with Matthew. Why confuse the children with all these Gospels? Let's go just with Matthew." But no, an effusive, ubiquitous, plenitudinous, and overflowing God requires at least four Gospels to talk about God and Christ.

And one way the church has historically attempted to talk about God's plenitudinousness and effusiveness, God's ubiquitousness and loquaciousness, is through the Trinity. Don't think of the Trinity as some incomprehensible doctrine of the church, though God's plenitudinousness is beyond our comprehension. Think of the Trinity as our earnest, though groping attempt, somehow to put into words what has been revealed to us of the overflowing love of God.

Sometimes you hear people say, "Well, you are a Christian, and I am not, but the important thing is that we all try to believe and serve God. Right?"

Wrong.

Christians are not those who believe in some amorphous, vague concept of "god." Christians are those who believe that God is best addressed as Trinity. God is not simply a monad, "God." God is the Father, God is the Son, and God is the Holy Spirit. And these three are One.

We might have been able to say, at some early point, "Well, we all believe in the same God." However, we believe that God came to us as Jesus. We believe that Jesus is God in the flesh, the fullness of God. The one from Nazareth was as much of God as we ever hope to see. This crucified Jew was raised from the dead, which was Gods way of saying, "You wonder what I'm like? Here's what I'm like—crucified, suffering, forgiving love."

And after experiencing that, all of our notions of God had to go back to the drawing table. If Jesus Christ is God, then we have a challenge in talking about God. After Easter, it just wouldn't do to talk about God as anything less than Trinity. In the Trinity Christians attempt to account for the complex biblical testimony that (1) God is always completely transcendent and omnipotent; and yet (2) Jesus, who died horribly and was raised miraculously by God, was somehow fully God; and that (3) the Spirit, poured out on the church, is also God; and yet (4) there is only one God.

The Trinity is our concept of where and how God gives God's self to be known, experienced, recognized, acknowledged, and obeyed as God. What impresses me about the New Testament's rare, explicit reference to the Trinity in Matthew 28 is the Risen Christ's statement: "I am with you always." Is this to be taken as a promise or a threat? This is said to the disciples, those who best knew Jesus, who had been with him throughout his ministry and therefore knew firsthand what a threat a fully present Jesus was to their existence. Therefore, is it good news or bad to be told, by the Christ, in effect, "I only had a few years to harass you before I was killed, but now that I am raised I am with you always"?

CHAPTER THREE

BIBLE

The Bible is demanding literature, not only because it is ancient literature written in languages other than our own but also because it commands obedience, response, and enactment. Therefore, the Bible requires being read "constantly" and "regularly"—"all" of it. To modern readers, accustomed to rather linear, flat narratives that neatly fit into our limited definitions of reality, the Bible can come across to us as a mess. To be sure, one encounters inconsistencies and contradictions, to say nothing of downright bad ideas in the Bible.

Scripture has a marvelous way of arguing with itself, correcting itself, one witness giving countertestimony to another. Scripture is a record of a people's determination to hear God truthfully and then to follow God faithfully. The record is in the form of a journey through many centuries. Scripture is the account of the adventure of a journey, not a report on having arrived at a destination. Might I also point out that we ourselves are a mess of inconsistencies, contradictions, and bad ideas? Most of the time it's much easier to see the cultural and historical limitations of the people in the Bible rather than in ourselves. We are still on the journey. It's not a simple song that the Bible wants to teach us to sing. It is a grand symphony that must be heard together with all of its highs and lows, its seemingly dissonant notes that all somehow come together and move in a definite direction.

The attempt to "get behind the text" acts as if the text is something to be shattered in order to get through the obfuscation of the text to what the text "really says." This is the preacher who announces, "Now what Jesus was trying to say in the parable of the prodigal son is..." No. What Jesus was trying to say is the parable. If one removes the form of the text, attempts to abstract some generalized concept or principle from behind the narrative, the result is something less than the narrative. The literary form has a function, a meaning that is irreplaceable by some other more abstract meaning.

Modernity tends toward reductionism; the Bible revels in thick, multilayered readings. Modernity, that mode of thinking whose ultimate goal is complete certainty and an unimpeded grasp of the facts, fostered a way of reading that moved toward the "point" of the text. I have argued here for a break with modernity, an admission of our inability to come to a clear, sure certitude about everything—including God's Word.

Modern methods of interpretation are frustrated by Scripture's delight in a cacophony of voices. The Bible tends not to speak in a unified, univocal way. Rather, the Bible presents a whole range of stories, often providing a variety of commentaries on those stories, sometimes reading them in quite different ways within the Bible itself. One can see this going on with the various interpretations of Jesus within the Gospels. Jesus is said to be the Messiah, God's anointed one. Yet he frustrates those expectations. He seems intent on rearranging, reinterpreting the very expectations he says he is fulfilling.

What is God like? A man had two sons. (It is known by us as "The Prodigal Son," although Jesus doesn't give his parables titles.) The younger son says, "Father, give me my inheritance." In other words, drop dead. (Is there any other way to put the old man's will into effect?) And the father does just that. Here we see an image of maturation which is most congenial to our society. America was built by immigrants, people who left their parents to seek their fortunes in this "far country" of a New World. And they, in turn, taught their children that the only way to get anywhere was to immigrate, to leave home, and to sever parental ties.

Out in the "far country," Jesus says the boy engages in "loose living." Pause just a moment to allow your imagination to work with that phrase, "loose living." Though Jesus doesn't, feel free to supply whatever forms of "loose living" appeal to you—loose girls, loose boys, chocolate cake.

With all the money wasted on loose living, the young man is reduced to the level of a pig. Imagine him in rags, swilling the pig slop to his porcine comrades. Eventually, it was hangover, empty pockets, wake-up time, Monday morning. The boy "comes to himself." He says, "Wait a minute. I don't have to starve out here. I have a father, a home."

And he turns back toward home. He has written a little speech for the occasion. "Now look, Dad. Before you start yelling, let me explain why she answered the phone when you called my room," or "Dad, er, uh, I mean, Father, I have sinned. I am unworthy to be called your son. Treat me as one of your hired servants."

But the father isn't interested in speeches.

"Chill, Howard," says the father. "Save the flowery speeches for your application to law school. Come on in. I'll show you a real party."

Which is why this story has always been a shocker. We thought Jesus came to jack up ethical standards, to put a bit more muscle into our moral fiber. Here is the homecoming of a ne'er-do-well as a party. It isn't what we expect. We want the father to be gracious, but not overly so. Homecomings for prodigals are fine, when prodigals are dressed in sackcloth and ashes, not in patent leather pumps and a tux. Our question is the same as that of the older brother, "Is it fitting to throw a party for a prodigal?"

It's a parable about a party thrown by a father for a prodigal. Jesus, in telling this story, expends more verses describing the party than on any other aspect in the story.

Put this parable in context. One day, Jesus' critics cried, "This man eats and drinks (that is, parties) with sinners! What kind of Savior are you?"

You expect Jesus to back off, saying, "I'm going to redeem these whores and tax collectors! Make 'em straighten up, be more responsible and middle class, like you and me."

No. He tells them that God loves to party with sinners, tells them parables of a party when a woman found a lost coin, and a bash after a shepherd found a lost sheep, followed by the biggest, most questionable blow-out of all—the party for the prodigal son. So, "they began to make merry." In the return of the wayward son from the "far country," Jesus dramatizes a return from exile. Israel's long deportation is ending. Come home, and join the great kingdom party! End of Scene One.

Scene Two: Now the music shifts from James Brown to Buxtehude, and in comes, in grand procession, the Dean of Students, Trustee Committee on Student Behavior, and Chair of the Judicial Board, all escorting their favorite character in the story—the older brother.

Nostrils flared, looks of indignation: "Music! Dancing! Levity! And on a Wednesday! What are you doing in that tux?" the older brother asks the servant.

"Your kid brother's home. The old man has given everybody the night off, and there's a party."

"A party! Doesn't that old fool know that we've got turnips to dig? How does he expect me to keep down overhead when he goes and wastes two grand on a party to welcome home this son of his who blew his hard-earned money on whores?"

Wait a second. When Jesus was telling the story earlier, did he say anything about whores? All he said was that the younger son blew his money in the far country on "loose living." Perhaps all that means is that he slept in late and ate high-cholesterol snacks.

But see? The converse of the older brother's, "See what a good boy am I," is always, "See what this son of yours has done . . . harlots, whores!"

The older son was angry and wouldn't go in. The father comes out into the darkness and begs him to come to the party.

"Lo, these many years have I served you," the older son sneers to the old man, "turning your turnip business around, putting the books in the black."

"Come on in, Ernest," says the father. "So what? You're the biggest turnip grower in Des Moines. Big deal. At least your kid brother has been to the city and tasted the wine. Come on in. Let's party."

As it turns out, the most interesting character in the story is not the prodigal son or the older brother. It's the father. He's the real prodigal because his love is extravagant, more excessive than either the younger brother's loose living or the older brother's moral rectitude. It's a story about a parent who is excessive in his persistence to have a family, an old man who meets us when we drag in from the far country after good times go bad and who comes out to the lonely dark of our righteousness and begs us to come in and party. It's a hopeful, joyous story of homecoming; it's a somber warning to those who would rather sulk in the dark than come in and join the homecoming dance.

"You are always with me. Everything I've got is yours," pleads the father out in the dark with the older brother. The father is willing to miss the first dance in the hope that his firstborn might relent his vaunted self-righteousness and join the party.

The Bible never questions: "Is there a God?" The Bible's question is: "Who is the God who is there?" John says that nobody has ever seen God until we met the one who told this parable. God is the long-suffering parent who waits for the younger son to come home when good times go bad and who also pleads with the older boy to come in, hug his brother, resume the family, and "make merry." The story's claim that God is the parent who refuses to stop silently waiting or earnestly pleading for you collides with modern self-understanding that our lives are our possessions, like a Chevrolet, to do with as we please. We are owned, the story implies, sought, even loved. The story also collides with the modern view of God as a detached, rule-driven, distant potentate who can't stand for the kids to have a good time.

Jesus' story doesn't have an ending. We are not told if the younger brother ever grew up and bought a Buick or if the older brother ever loosened up and joined the party. We doubt that they "lived happily ever after." (I told you this was a true story.) Jesus doesn't end the story, because this is the kind of story which you finish yourself. And you do, even if you don't know it. I'm betting that the one whom the father is awaiting, the one whom he is begging to come in and party, is you. This story says: you journey not alone. There is One who names you, claims you, has plans for you, waits or prods, invites, or blesses you. This One, sooner or later, will have you.

God's realm is at once so very strange—like a thief in the night, seed growing secretly, undeserved miraculous harvest, treasure in a field—and at the same time, so very close, ordinary, and real—like seed, weeds, fish, and shady business deals. The kingdom is that realm ruled by the God who manages to be at once so close to us and also quite far from us, a God we could never have thought up without outrageous parables. The truth about God is a truth that is comprehended only parabolically. Jesus almost never sounds like us preachers—full of principles, platitudes, pronouncements, three-point sermons, eternal, absolute, unarguable assertions. Jesus' truth is concrete, close to the stuff of daily life, yet enigmatic, beyond daily life, ambiguous, open to debate, demanding rumination and interpretation.

That dark night when Jesus was arrested, the disciples, in an attempt to save their own skins, flee into the darkness. Mark says that a "young man" who was with them is grabbed by one of the soldiers, and he too flees into the darkness, naked, leaving a surprised soldier holding nothing but the youth's robe.

Who is that naked man? What was he up to? Why would Mark mention him here, at this climactic moment in the story of Jesus? Early commentators speculated that the young man was one of the unnamed disciples. Some said he was a prefigurement of Jesus—just as Jesus shortly will give death the slip, leaving his shroud in the tomb, so the young man has given death the slip—an advance sign of the coming resurrection. Truth is, nobody has any idea why he was there.

I love these unexplained, unusable events in the story that remind us that we may come to know and love Jesus, but we will never, ever control, grasp, or hold on to Jesus anymore than the soldiers capture that young streaker.

I've spent my whole adult life studying the parabolic teachings of Jesus. And yet I confess that, to this day, I really don't know for sure why Jesus told the parable of the dishonest manager who swindled his boss and who, in turn, was goofily praised by his boss. I don't know what to do with such a patently absurd story. Why, Jesus?

Perhaps I'm not to do anything with the story or the rabbi who dared to tell it to a nice, cautious, rational person like me. Maybe, in telling this story, the rabbi is trying to do something with me.

──◁▨▷── ──◁▨▷── ──◁▨▷── ──◁▨▷── ──◁▨▷──

A farmer goes forth to sow seed and—carefully, meticulously—prepares the ground, removing all rocks and weeds, sowing one seed six inches from another? No. The farmer, without prepara-tion, begins slinging seed. A dragnet is hauled into the boat full of creatures both good and bad. Should the catch be sorted, sep-arating the good from the bad? No. The Master is more impressed with the size of the haul than with the quality of the harvest. One day, not today, it will all be sorted.

A field is planted with good seed. But a perverse enemy sows weeds in the field. Should we cull the wheat from the weeds? No. The Master says that someday he will judge good from bad, but we are not to bother ourselves with such sorting today. The Master seems to be more into careless sowing, miraculous growing, and reckless harvesting than in taxonomy of the good from the bad, the worthwhile from the worthless, the saved from the damned.

"Which one of you?" to paraphrase Jesus' questions in Luke 15, "having lost one sheep will not leave the ninety-nine sheep to fend for themselves in the wilderness and beat the bushes until you find the one lost sheep? Which one of you will not put that sheep on your shoulders like a lost child and say to your friends, 'Come party with me'? Which one of you would not do that?"

"Which of you women," Jesus continues, "if you lose a quarter will not rip up the carpet and strip the house bare and when you have found your lost coin run into the street and call to your neighbors, 'Come party with me, I found my quarter!' Which one of you would not do that?"

And which of you fathers, having two sons, the younger of whom leaves home, blows all your money, comes dragging back home in rags, will not throw the biggest bash this town has ever seen, singing, "This son of mine was dead but is now alive!" Which one of you would not do that?

And which of you, journeying down the Jericho Road, upon seeing a perfect stranger lying in the ditch half dead, bleeding, would not risk your life, put the injured man in the backseat of your Jaguar, take him to the hospital, spend every dime you have on his recovery, and more. Which of you would not do that?

The answer is that *none of us* would behave in this unseemly, reckless, and extravagant way. These are not stories about us. These are God's stories—God the searching shepherd, the careless farmer, the undiscerning fisherman, the reckless woman, the extravagant father, the prodigal Samaritan. Jesus thus reveals a God who is no discrete minimalist. Abundance is in the nature of this God. So when Jesus, confronted by the hunger of the multitudes (Mark 8), took what his disciples had and blessed it, there was not only enough to satisfy the hungry ones but also a surplus, more than enough. Jesus demonstrates a surfeit that is at the heart of all God-given reality.

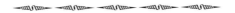

Karl Barth tells us what the gospel is not—it is not religious experience, not moral platitudes, not an attempt to straighten out the world, not a deeper appreciation of nature, not something personal and subjective, not ancient history—in order to say that salvation is "the mighty acts of God in history for the liberation of the cosmos." The first book of the Bible says that the world is initiated solely through an act of God and the last book of the Bible is a sustained hymn that sings the great triumph of God in which creatures in heaven and on earth sing that "salvation belongs to our God who is seated on the throne" (Rev 7:10). Crucified Jesus is the one who brings, "Salvation and glory and power" (Rev 19:1).

A Christian is someone who lives in the light of this story. A Christian and a Buddhist (or for that matter, a Republican or a Democrat) differ primarily on the basis of the stories they are living. These stories tell us what is going on in the world, what we might reasonably expect and who really sits on the throne.

When we say that the Bible is "true," we mean that the Bible's way of narrating the world is truthful. The Bible's means of making meaning is trustworthy. Its way of understanding and constructing the world is faithful to things as they are, and in God's good time, shall be.

The truth of any statement depends upon what it means, as well as the way it means what it means. Different literary genres have different ways of making meaning. If I say, "What's in a name? That which we call a rose by any other name would smell as sweet," is this statement true? It's truthfulness depends on the sort of literature employed and the way it means what it means. The statement is a quotation from *Romeo and Juliet*. If it were a theory being proposed by a biologist, or a press release from a government official, that would make a difference.

If, through historical research, it could be shown that *Romeo and Juliet* is not historically accurate, that the Capulets were not as belligerent as they are portrayed in Shakespeare's play, who cares? Different genres of literature play by different rules. If I were to say, "There was once this traveling salesman, see? And he came upon this farmhouse and . . ." You are hearing a clue, a code. You are probably about to hear a tasteless joke. You would apply different rules for interpretation than if I were to begin in the jargon of contractual law by saying, "Whereas the party of the first part, in consideration for the sum of fifty dollars from the party of the second part. . . ."

One of the challenges of biblical interpretation is that the Bible contains a wide array of genre. We contemporary preachers of the Word marvel at the resourcefulness of these early communicators of the faith. They use poetry, myth, parable, genealogy, invective, hyperbole, and a host of other literary devices and conventions to communicate the truth about God. We do them a disservice when we apply inappropriate standards of interpretation to the literature that they employ.

Theologian William Placher once noted that when we read the

story of the good Samaritan in Luke, no one needs to check a police blotter from the Jerusalem to Jericho highway patrol to understand the story. If we find the story difficult to understand, it will not be because there is some historical problem with the story. Jesus tells this story to initiate a theological transformation, so the challenge to our understanding will be theological rather than historical. As it has been noted, Genesis may not be scientifically true. It is eternally true. It is making a claim not so much about how the world came to be, but about *who* enabled the world to be.

Fortunately, biblical texts often provide clues that enable us to identify their genre and thus aid in their interpretation. If the rabbi says, "The kingdom of God is like…" we are going to hear a simile, something is going to be compared to something else. "In those days there went out a decree from Caesar Augustus.…" It sounds like we are going to read history, because a historical figure is being named. The Bible enjoys often employing a history-like genre in which historical people and places are mentioned in order to give a sense of time and place to the story, in order to give the narrative more location than the merely "once upon a time."

When we read apocalyptic literature in Daniel or Revelation, we are reading a specific genre that has its own conventions and rules for reading. "Apocalyptic" comes from the Greek, meaning "to uncover" or "to reveal." In these strange, gripping images, we are meant to see something that we could not see without the aid of the images. We cannot peel away the layers of metaphor and get the literature down to some abstract theological statement without doing damage to the intent of the literature. There can be no "demythologizing" (Bultmann) that does not end up with something considerably less than the "myth" intends.

We tend to delude ourselves into thinking that we have difficulty with biblical literature, such as apocalyptic, because we are sophisticated and modern, whereas apocalyptic is primitive. But as modern people we are caught in a constricting social location that limits our ability to understand. Apocalyptic is often difficult to understand, not because the literature is communicating in some primitive secret code, but rather because the literature of apocalyptic is attempting to get us to look at something that it is difficult for us to see. This is, namely, that God, not nations, rules the world; that the end of the world is in God's hands, not ours; and that God shall bring all things to fulfillment in accordance with God's purposes. In other words, many of our interpretive problems are more political than linguistic in origin. We say that Jesus' healing miracles are a problem for sophisticated, scientific people like us. What we may mean is that we no longer look to God for our healing. We believe in medicine rather than miracle. Medicine is our major means of achieving immortality, healing, and a life free of pain. So when we make a judgment about what can and what cannot be, what is possible and impossible, our judgments are also testimonials to the sort of world in which we think we live, the sort of gods whom we serve.

We are not taking apocalyptic more seriously when we attempt to apply this literature to our own day, attempting a one-to-one correlation between the supposed events described there and specific politics of our own day. When we fail to take biblical literature on its own terms, we abuse the Bible and fail to respect its own distinctive voices and the rich, resourceful array of genres that biblical writers use in order to communicate the truth. The result is spiritual starvation.

We are modern people who have been taught by our culture to believe that we are privileged to stand upon the very summit of human development. From our serene contemporary perch we stand in judgment on everyone who got here before us. We have progressed. We are making progress. We know so much more than they. To affirm that Scripture, "both in the Old and New Testament," is a reliable, unsubstitutable guide for our salvation, our future with God, is to go against modern prejudice. We look for God and listen for God with these ancient witnesses who have gone before us. We do our best to allow the various voices within the canon of Scripture to share their distinctive testimonies with us. Fortunately, we need not reinvent the wheel in regard to Christian discipleship. If we will dare listen, the saints will show us the way.

To say that Scripture ought to be read as a whole puts at rest the unfortunate stereotype that has demeaned the Old Testament, playing it off against the New with slogans such as, "The Old Testament is a collection of laws and judgment; the New Testament contains books of love and grace." Wesley found grace in many parts of the Hebrew Scriptures, and he strongly believed (against some in the Protestant Reformation, that is, Luther) that God's law was a sign of God's gracious, loving determination not to leave us alone to make do with our own devices. He rejected any simplistic or wooden law-versus-gospel distinction.

Wesley therefore taught that it is wrong to lift out of context a single passage of Scripture, attempting to read that passage isolated from other relevant passages. Scripture interprets Scripture and cumulatively points toward God's love and care.

Prooftexting—searching for one passage that proves your pet doctrine or disproves your neighbor's pet doctrine—is an abuse of Scripture's unity and "general tenor." All passages of Scripture must be read in the context of the whole story that God is telling us through Scripture. Martin Luther was fond of saying that the Bible is like the swaddling clothes that were wrapped around the baby Jesus, the manger in which Christ was laid. We don't worship the Bible; we worship the Savior to whom all Scripture—in diverse ways—testifies. All Scripture, Old Testament and New, points to and is to be evaluated by the supreme revelation of God, the Incarnate Word—Jesus Christ.

The God of Scripture has this wonderful way of showing up just as we thought the story was ending, and by showing up, continuing the story, giving the story a more interesting ending than the drama would have had, had there not been a God who loves to raise the dead. A large degree of optimism is warranted by the biblical evidence.

A farmer needs workers for his vineyard (Matthew 20). So he arises early, goes out and finds some willing workers to harvest his grapes, agreeing with them on the usual daily wage. An invitation has been offered and accepted. End of story.

But as is so often with Jesus, it isn't the end of the story. Midmorning we are surprised to find the farmer back downtown, hiring more workers for his vineyard, agreeing to pay them "what's right." At noon, mid-afternoon, *one hour before quitting time*, the farmer is out wheeling and dealing, seemingly unable to rest until everyone in town is working in his vineyard. And Jesus says, God's kingdom is like that.

Peter, the premier disciple, in the Upper Room, at the end, promises, "Though everyone else desert you, I will not desert you!" Jesus predicts that Peter will fall away before morning. The soldiers appear and drag Jesus away for death. Peter, with the others, scurries away. Midnight finds him warming himself by a charcoal fire. There a little serving girl asks him about Jesus and devastates his resolve. Peter denies Jesus not once but thrice and melts into tears at his failure.

Sometime later Peter and the other disciples have returned to fishing. In the morning, as the sun rises, they see a figure on the beach, cooking over a charcoal fire. He graciously invites Peter to breakfast. It is none other than the Lord who presides over this meal. And then the Lord looks into this betrayer's face and commissions him to "feed my sheep." The story isn't over until God says it's over.

God is like that.

Once upon a time, there was a rich man (and you know how we despise the rich) who got word that his manager was pilfering from him. So he summoned the little guy for an audit.

"What's this I hear? Show me the books!"

"Er, Boss, uh, nothin' would please me more than to show you the books—I need to do a few...calculations."

The little weasel thinks to himself, "I'm too proud to beg and too weak to do any real work. What am I to do? I've got it! I'll call in my master's debtors and have them write down their debts. They'll be so grateful that, when my master sacks me, I can go to them for help."

Thus, the swindle begins. Each of the debtors is called in and asked, "You owe the master $1,000? Let's mark that down to $250. How you like them numbers?"

Huge sums of money are written off.

Then comes the day of judgment. Now the little wretch will get what his thievery deserves. The dishonest manager presents the cooked books to the master. The master responds with, "You...you *genius* you! Wow! What wonderful initiative. What commercial creativity. What innovative book keeping. I wish all my people were as smart in looking after their future."

Now, what kind of Savior would have told a story like that to people like us? (Yep, he really did tell this story.)

Did you hear the one about the man traveling from Jerusalem to Jericho who was mugged, beaten, stripped naked, and left to die like a dog in a ditch?

Now, by chance, down the road comes a priest, a religious official, a man who makes his living off of God—and you know how we all despise clergy. He espies the man bleeding, lying helpless in the ditch, and the priest...passes by on the other side.

Then comes down the road a pious but not priggish, religious but not showy, ordinary Methodist person who, catching a whiff of the now putrefying mess in the ditch, and being religious and therefore quite a cautious sort of person...passes by on the other side.

Imagine you are the man in the ditch. You've lost a lot of blood. Time is running out. With your last ounce of energy you look down that hot, dusty road and see coming toward you—a nice-looking, spiritual but not fanatical, probably Republican, traditional-values person like you? No. You see a despised, good-for-nothing, racially impure, theologically uninformed *Samaritan*. Your last best hope is a man whom you hate.

And despite your weak protests—"it's only a flesh wound. I'm OK, I'm OK"—this lousy Samaritan rips up his designer suit, lays your bleeding carcass on the fine leather seats of his Porsche, takes you to the hospital, shells out all of his credit cards, and tells them to spare no expense in your salvation.

"Go and do likewise," says Jesus.

Is this a joke? Parables, these pithy, strange little stories from everyday life, are the most distinctive—and peculiar—aspect of the teaching of Jesus. Parables are close cousins of another distinctive literary form: the joke. Mark says that Jesus never said anything in public that wasn't a parable. There are religious teachers who, when asked a theological question, respond with thoughtful, general principles, high-sounding, serious and uplifting. Muhammad and Dr. Phil leap to mind.

Why, Jesus? Why do you explain God with unexplained stories, most of which lack neat endings or immediately apparent points? It's as if Jesus says that God is not met through generalities and abstractions; God is met amid the stuff of daily life, in the tug and pull of the ordinary. Yet God is usually encountered, if the parables have it right, in ways that are rarely self-evident, obvious, or with uncontested meaning. In parables, the joke is on us.

⚡ ⚡ ⚡ ⚡ ⚡

Scripture delights in a surplus of meaning; it revels in eluding our interpretive grasp. Even after we have applied our very best and most reliable methods of interpretation, there is still more to be said about a given text, still more meaning to be spoken, still something left over to be revealed to us upon later reading, still one more sermon to be preached on "the real meaning of Christmas," thank God. Thus Scripture engenders interpretive humility, particularly among modern people who enjoy grasping and comprehending everything. Indeed, the very elusiveness of some Scripture is itself an encouragement, a catalyst to human imagination, teasing us toward itself, beckoning us to use our God-given abilities to decipher and to understand. Thus Karl Barth compared the style of Genesis to the vast, too rich, uncontainable novels of Fyodor Dostoyevsky.

Scripture requires the activity of the Holy Spirit to speak. Words become the Word by the empowering presence and activity of the Holy Spirit. Modernity taught that most rational human beings, regardless of background, training, or character, were perfectly capable of unaided understanding, perfectly able to grasp and comprehend everything in the world simply by the use of reason. Scripture frustrates such limited knowing. Scripture opens itself up to us through the work of the Holy Spirit, whom we cannot rationalize or control, and modernity is high on control and rationalization. Thus, interpretation of Scripture is a communal, pneumatic affair—a work of grace—requiring considerably more than the lone, reasoning reader.

We would know nothing about the Trinity, redemption in Jesus, or the work of grace through the Holy Spirit if God had not given us Scripture. Christian doctrine is a product of the church's encounter with a group of ancient writings that were compiled over a four thousand-year period, none of which are younger than nearly two thousand years. The church is sustained, encouraged, and at the same time severely criticized and challenged by the very same Scripture that the church produced. We meet Christ in Scripture in a way that is singular and fecund. In our encounters with Scripture we believe we hear the voice, see the ways, and receive the guidance of the living God.

Scripture was produced by communities of faith who had experienced God's presence and interaction with them in vivid ways. Something undeniable and real had happened to them, and now they wanted to tell everyone the news. Not that all their testimony was uniform or rendered in the same way. In fact, some of the diversity of the testimony is a sort of proof that the events they were trying to relate were so mind-boggling and boundary-breaking that they were very difficult to put into speech. We are the beneficiaries of their testimony; we are the result of the encounter that their testimony provokes in each succeeding generation:

> We declare to you..., what we have heard, what we have seen..., what we have...touched with our hands, concerning the word of life....We declare to you what we have seen and heard so that you also may have fellowship with us; and truly our fellowship is with the Father and with his Son Jesus Christ. We are writing these things so that our joy may be complete. (1 John 1:1-4)

It is a principle of faithful Christian doctrine that we try hard to make no theological statement that does not arise out of and is in turn answerable to Scripture. In theology, ideas and concepts that can claim no other source than fertile human imagination are otherwise known as heresy—God talk that originates in ourselves rather than in Scripture. That's one reason why after the Articles of Religion speak of God—Father, Son, and Holy Spirit—the very next topic is "Of the Sufficiency of the Holy Scriptures for Salvation," a statement that claims that the Bible "containeth all things necessary to salvation." Lest you think of theology as a complicated affair, something that you can never hope to figure out, Article 5 reassures you that everything anyone really needs to know in order to be with God is graciously given in the Bible. We need not rummage around elsewhere for revelation. It's all here, more than we'll ever be able to process in a lifetime of sermons, all that we need to know of God and more.

Today, when popular novels and movies come forth claiming to have exposed some secret knowledge, a story of some sinister church plot that has now been revealed, it's good to know that, while such claims sometimes make for a good story, the church loves us enough to reassure us that there are not two classes of Christians—those who have been let in on the secret knowledge and those benighted souls who have yet to find the hidden key. All struggling believers are reassured: God's revelation is not rare, arcane, and obtuse. What God is doing for us and what God promises us and what God expects of us, all is fully revealed in Scripture.

The gap between the cultures of the Bible and our own does make some, but not all, scriptural applications difficult. Sometimes there is a tendency to focus on those passages that are questionable and difficult, and ignore those that are all too clear in their directives. Jesus appears to have been relatively straightforward in his condemnation of marriage after divorce, though it is also clear that early Christian interpreters struggled with his condemnation, and so do we. We struggle to interpret some difficult passages, not simply because we want to weasel out of the Bible's plain demands, but also because we know that sometimes Scripture corrects Scripture. Within the canon is an ongoing argument with itself over certain subjects. In Matthew's Gospel, Jesus often pronounces, "You have heard it said [in Scripture], but I say to you..." Most scholars see the book of Job as an extended argument of the smug equation of good works equaling easy lives that occurs in some of the Wisdom Literature. Scripture interprets Scripture.

From Scripture, the church is given more than directives, rules, codes for contemporary Christian behavior. The main gift of Scripture is a world, a culture, a reality constructed (as all worlds, cultures, and reality are fabricated) through words. Words make the world. In the beginning, God created the world through the Word. The world belongs to those who name reality truthfully. Christians are those who, through Scripture, are taught to name the world, not merely as "nature," but rather as "Creation." We learn to name our lives not as under the grip of fate, or luck, but as guided and cared for by providence. We do not make "mistakes." We sin. We do not want to be improved. We hope for salvation.

The Bible has a privileged place in our communication. We are not free, as the church, to rummage about among other authorities, sources of inspiration, and revelation until we have first been encountered by Scripture. To be a Christian means to be someone who learns to lay one's life alongside the biblical text, allowing the text to serve as canon or rule ("canon" means literally "ruler," or "yardstick") for how one gets on in the world. In that primal, originating act—that which we read of in Nehemiah or Luke 4, where the text is set against us in order that we might more faithfully read ourselves into the text, where the Word is read and interpreted and the people respond—is the origin and the sustenance of the people of God who become that way by being the people of the Book.

<hr/>

To read Scripture is to read an account of a work in progress. In a sense, the validity and the authority of Scripture are rightly judged by the quality of lives that Scripture is able to produce. Our claim is not so much that Scripture is relevant or useful to our lives (goodness knows, we will enlist almost anything in our efforts to set ourselves up on our terms rather than God's), but that through Scripture, the living God speaks to us and transforms us.

In reading the Bible like Wesleyans, we do not ask, "Is this relevant to my life?" Instead we assume the stance of our parents in the faith before us and say, "Speak, LORD, for your servant is listening" (1 Sam. 3:9). The question is the potentially transforming one of, "How might my life be made more relevant to the work that Christ wants to do in the world?" We cannot affirm that Jesus Christ is Lord without obeying him as our Sovereign, without placing ourselves at his disposal, without hearing his word as our summons. Rarely does the Bible cooperate with our search for quick, easy answers or clear, simple ideas of God; Scripture has a way of complicating our notions of God and teaching us to ask even more demanding questions.

Second Timothy states that "all scripture is inspired by God and is useful for teaching, for reproof, for correction, and for training in righteousness," which makes the Bible sound rather close to a rulebook for doctrinal policing. But then the writer adds, "So that everyone...may be...equipped for every good work" (3:16-17)—a wonderfully Wesleyan statement of the function and goal of our times with the sacred text.

The church is never-ending training in learning to trust the Bible, learning to take ourselves a little less seriously and the Bible a bit more so. We gather on Sunday, the Scriptures are opened to the church, we say, "Let's all believe that this ancient book—written in a time and a language quite different from our own, by a people in many ways different from us—knows more than we." Then we attend to Scripture. Bending our lives toward the text that reaches out to us through a wide array of literary devices, thus the church is forever formed, reformed into the church of Christ.

We trust the Bible in much the same way that we learn to trust another person. William Placher notes that when you trust someone, you know them and allow them to know you. You spend time with that person, some of it with serious intent, some of it simply to be with that person. When you converse together, because you have learned to know and to trust one another, you know that person's jokes as jokes, their tall tales as tall tales, their admonitions as words addressed to you out of love. Although we may not understand everything about that person, may not be able to connect everything that is said to us by our friend, we learn to trust that person as having our best interests at heart. We trust that we will not be led astray. We take some delight that our friend, even when we may have known her for many years, is still able to shock, surprise, and confuse us, because such shock and surprise remind us of the delightful, mysterious, not fully comprehensible otherness of our friend.

We trust the Bible because it keeps making sense of, as well as disrupting, the world in which we live. The Bible does not just "make sense" in the sense that the Bible is congruent with our present experiences of and definitions of reality. We must read the Bible in a way that is more careful and respectful than simply going to the Bible, rummaging about, picking and choosing on the basis of what we consider to be possible and permissible within our present context. To do so is not to align our lives with the witness of the saints, but rather to, in Barth's words, "adorn ourselves with their feathers." The temptation is to discard that which makes us uncomfortable or that which does not easily fit into our present conceptual scheme of things. Therefore, an appropriate hermeneutical question is not simply, What does this text mean? but rather, How is this text asking me to change?

I read in the newspaper of a woman—I think she lived in Louisiana—who had raised about a dozen foster children despite her meager income as a domestic worker. Why did she do it? She replied, "I saw a new world a-comin'."

To read Scripture is to risk transformation, conversion, an exchange of masters. You might think of Sunday morning as a struggle over the question, Who tells the story of what is going on in the world? Scripture reading can be uncomfortable, as we are made by the Bible to see things we would have just as soon ignored, as we hear a word we have been trying to avoid. Reading is not only a formative activity but also a potentially disruptive means of exiting our culture, of defamiliarizing and making the normal seem strange and the strange seem normal, of having a delightful respite from conventional, culturally sanctioned accounts of "the way things are." Therefore, the primary interpretive question is not, "Do I understand this passage?" but rather, "How is this text attempting to convert me to Christ?" Behind all Scripture is not simply the question, "Will you agree?" but rather the more political, "Will you join up?"

CHAPTER FOUR

BAD NEWS

In Augustine's *Confessions*, Book II, the infamous episode about the stealing of the pears, Augustine magnifies a sin that seems so inconsequential. By this time in the account of his life, Augustine has fathered a child out of wedlock, has hinted at many youthful indiscretions. And yet when he comes to the prime example of his deep perversity, he gives as evidence the stealing of a few pears. Is Augustine being overscrupulous?

Augustine was notoriously convinced of his own great sinfulness. He presents adolescence as a time when "I cared for nothing but to love and be loved" (2.2). The theft of pears by a group of boys may not seem to us like a great sin, but it becomes for Augustine a revelation of the way in which his problem is not simply the sins that he commits, but his inclination toward sin. He finds that the human being is fascinated with some actions simply because the actions are illicit and prohibited.

He and some friends steal a few pears from a neighbor's pear tree, not because they are hungry or need to steal the pears, but from *eo liberet quo non liceret,* "that which is not permitted allured us," which is to say, just for the hell of it. The important thing is not the transgression, for perhaps Augustine intends for the transgression to be pointedly of minor moral significance. Rather the problem is the inclination, the desire.

I've spent most of my life trying to figure out what I'm doing. Isn't that how they defined "human growth" in that child development class? "Human growth is the process of increasing self-awareness"?

We begin with naked instinct, mechanical reaction, hormonal response, but gradually, with puberty and a college education, gradually we learn where we are and what we're doing. We learn to seek pleasure and to avoid pain. We learn to avoid certain unproductive, dysfunctional behavior and to engage in more fruitful, beneficial conduct, and, now possessed with a keen sense of "self-awareness" we move reflectively, knowledgeably about the world, "our" world that, through our knowledge, we have made our own.

Yeah, right.

I took a course in seminary in Christian ethics. Christian ethics is the weighing of various ethical options and, through careful, rational deliberation, discerning the one right action and then pursuing that option in a prudential way.

Yeah, right.

I made an A in that course in rational ethical deliberation only to flunk when I tried actually to do that in life.

One little problem with our attempts to be thoughtful, prudent, reflective, and careful people: we're also the ones who on a Friday—just rationally following the best of Western jurisprudence—tortured to death the very Son of God.

Why? Well, we didn't know what we were doing. We did not then know, do not now know, will never know what we're doing. We're all stumbling in the dark. I once knew a man who, on sentry duty one dark night in France in the Second World War, was surprised to get a perfect shot of a German soldier coming toward him down a country road. When he went up to examine the body, he discovered it to be one of his best friends from another

52

unit. He did not seem to be much consoled by my, "But you didn't know what you were doing."

───◦───　───◦───　───◦───　───◦───　───◦───

Martin Luther extolled righteous anger as the engine that drove him on to some of his very best work. "I never work better than when I am inspired by anger; for when I am angry I can write, pray, and preach well, for then my whole temperature is quickened, my understanding sharpened, and all mundane vexations and temptations depart."

I know what Luther is talking about. When I was unjustly attacked (in my opinion) by a right-wing religious hate group, a victim of their hateful e-mails and venom, I sat down and wrote one of the most unfair, direct, fierce, unkind articles I've ever published. I thought it also one of my best. Anger is a powerful human motivating force for good, says Jesus as he boots the clergy out of the Temple.

And yet…anger, in our hands, righteous indignation practiced by us, is a dangerous thing. Martin Luther's obscene denunciations of the Jews were written under the influence of anger. Anger tends to drive us, zeal to right what's wrong with us and the world, but rather even deeper into ourselves, in seething, simmering resentment. Part of its sin is isolation. We are right, the world is wrong. We are victims of injustice, the world is unjust. Luther defined sin as "the heart all curved in on itself." Anger is famous for beginning with focus upon another and ending all curved in upon itself. If there is one thing worse than Anger enacted, it is anger nursed, turned inward, fed and nurtured.

I once taught a student who had been abused by her exhusband. I heard her story the first day of class when she told me that, due to her history of abuse, she had trouble with men as professors. Then the class heard about her victimization at every opportunity. Repeatedly we heard of her continuing resentment at what this man had done to her. Ten years ago! I had the unpleasant task of telling her that if she could not do something about that anger, she would never be able to function in ministry. There was no way that she could help others, until she first helped herself. I told her, "I never met your ex-husband and still I hate him—for his continuing abuse of you through the devastating effects of your anger."

Anger protects the status quo of the ego. Anger isolates us, keeps us from having to be affected by the world around us, from having to change. Perhaps that helps to explain why there are some people who appear to cling to their anger, lovingly to refurbish and nourish their anger, realizing that if they ever loose their grip upon anger (or dared to try to break free of anger's grip on them) they would be forced to be different.

A recent television documentary, entitled "The Changing Face of Worship" took us into dozens of growing, innovative, "postmodern" churches. Sunday at many of these churches struck me as almost unbearably upbeat, energetic, and positive, just what I expect from the well-furnished "Seeker-sensitive church." But one young pastor on the West Coast, leader of a burgeoning, mostly young adult congregation, when asked to explain why so many flocked to his services, said, "Too few young adults have had anyone look them in the face, and say directly to them, with a sense of concern and compassion, *'You really suck.'*"

I might have put the matter more elegantly, but I agree with him theologically. People are not as dumb as much of mainline, liberal Protestantism, or for that matter not as self-deceptive as allegedly evangelical, biblical conservatism, takes them to be. As C. S. Lewis noted, "It is the policy of the Devil to persuade us there is no Devil." It is a sure sign of a compromised church—a church that has retired from the battle with the principalities and powers, a church without prophets—when one finds a church that has stopped dealing with sin. Or, as a character in one of Oscar Wilde's plays says, "One should believe evil of everyone, until, of course, people are found out to be good. But that requires a great deal of investigation nowadays" (*A Woman of No Importance*).

When I openly marveled at the success of TV's "Dr. Phil," wondering why his Texas-direct, blunt-to-the-point-of-cruel talk got him such an audience, a psychotherapist in my congregation explained, "People are ready to be told the truth about themselves, even when it hurts, because they know that, without getting the truth, they won't get life." Even if we don't enjoy having the truth told directly to us, we do enjoy listening in as Dr. Phil tells the truth to someone else.

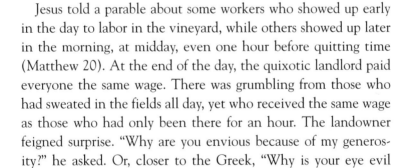

Jesus told a parable about some workers who showed up early in the day to labor in the vineyard, while others showed up later in the morning, at midday, even one hour before quitting time (Matthew 20). At the end of the day, the quixotic landlord paid everyone the same wage. There was grumbling from those who had sweated in the fields all day, yet who received the same wage as those who had only been there for an hour. The landowner feigned surprise. "Why are you envious because of my generosity?" he asked. Or, closer to the Greek, "Why is your eye evil (*opthalmos poneros*), because I am good?" Why begrudge the master's generosity?

I'll tell you why. Those of us who have been lifelong Christians, attempting to follow Jesus from our youth, bored to tears for decades in Sunday school and long sermons, why should we not be envious when some little wayward lamb staggers back to the sheepfold, or some once Prodigal Son turns back toward home? Our God is gracious, forgiving, abounding in mercy.

Grace, mercy, and forgiveness, when they are offered to you, can be just as envied by me, even more envied, than cars, money, and power. Grace, when it is so freely offered to any and all comers, without regard to my merit, especially when offered to latecomers, seems somehow less gracious than when it is reserved for me.

The first murder, a fratricide, that trouble between Cain and Abel, was due to Envy at the gracious love of God showered on a brother. Some animosity among religious people could be chalked up to the childish "my God is better than yours" attitude, but I wonder if some of that enmity is due to the "your god seems oddly more beneficent than mine" attitude. I expect that the blessings of God have led to more head bashing than any other source of Envy. Why God blessed the heathen Arabs with all that oil, I will never know.

━══◫◫◫══━ ━══◫◫◫══━ ━══◫◫◫══━ ━══◫◫◫══━ ━══◫◫◫══━

I recently heard a management guru declare, "There is no more important quality to cultivate among the workers in a company than pride in their products." Our political life seems dominated now by the politics of self-assertion, and our therapies are mostly the relentless psychology of vaunted self-esteem. The great sin for us is not Pride, but low self-image. Somehow Pride and its cousins—arrogance, egotism, vanity, and conceit—got trumped by self-respect, self-esteem, self-confidence, and self-ascribed dignity. Jesus' exhortation to "love thy neighbor as thyself" has been shortened to a hard and fast, ruthlessly enforced mandate: *love thyself!*

I am not so sure that low self-esteem is our greatest problem. Did the Nazis build on low German self-esteem in order to get power in Germany or just the opposite, building upon German delusions of national exceptionalism and Pride? I recall a conversation with a crusty old prison chaplain. I said something about all the people who were in jail because they suffered from a "warped sense of themselves," and he quickly corrected me. "That's horseshit. Those guys are not in jail because they think too little of themselves, but because they think too much of themselves. Every one of them thinks he's a brilliant mind who is above the poor saps who obey the rules, go to work, follow the law. Every one of them thinks he's a damn genius and his victims are stupid."

I asked a recovering alcoholic in my congregation, "Sam, why have you stopped coming to church?" He replied, "Preacher, after you have been to AA, and taken the cure, and had to stare your demons in the face, and had to stand up naked in front of twenty other drunks and tell every bad thing you have done or thought, and had to ask God and them to forgive you for being you, well, church just seems like such a trivial waste of time."

Church is about more than sin, but, by the grace of God, it ought not to be less than this.

It is of the prophetic ministry of the church to teach people that we are sinners. Think of church as lifelong learning in how to be a sinner. We may be conceived in sin, but we fail to be cognizant of sin without the grace of God. The "sins" of non-Christians tend to be rather puny. For Christians, sin is not so much inherent in the human condition, though it is that; rather, sin is the problem we have between us and God. It is rebellion against our true Sovereign, an offense against the way the Creator has created us to be. The gospel story that we are forgiven-being-redeemed sinners is the means whereby we are able to be honest about the reality, complexity, and perversity of our sin.

Christians are conditioned to name human self-assertion as a subspecies of the sin of idolatry, setting ourselves up as gods. What the world calls healthy "self-esteem," Christians sniff out as idolatry, self-worship. The devil in the desert had it right in telling Jesus that he could be empowered to set the world right, to correct all of God's mistakes at creation; all that was necessary was to "worship me" and "all this will be yours."

A member of our faculty recently justified to me his disbelief of Christianity by saying that "With all the suffering and pain in the world, I just can't see how you can call God good. I am very sensitive to the plight of others."

I'm sure that he thinks of himself as a humble, sincere disbeliever. Another way of looking at him is that he considers himself better, more sensitive, and more caring than the God who would make such a lousy world. If he—with his master's degree and his global sensitivity—had been God, he would have made a better world. It's the serpent's promise, "You will be like gods. . . ."

I've got a Jewish friend who is fond of saying, "Jews have two major beliefs: (1) there is a God; (2) you are not it."

The church's notion of sin, like that of Israel before it, is peculiar. It is derived, not from speculation about the universal or general state of humanity, but rather from a peculiar, quite specific account of what God is up to in the world. What God is up to is named as Covenant, Torah, or, for Christians, the Cross of Jesus. If we attempt to begin in Genesis, with Adam and Eve and their alleged "fall," we will be mistaken into thinking of sin as some innate, indelible glitch in human nature. We must start with Exodus rather than Genesis, with Sinai rather than the Garden of Eden, with Calvary. Only by getting the story straight—God's story of redemption—are we able to tell our stories truthfully. Christians believe that the only means of understanding our sin

with appropriate seriousness and without despair is our knowledge of a God who manages to be both gracious and truthful. Our
human situation is not that we are all dressed up with a will to
power and transcendence with nowhere to go but finitude and
failure. Our situation is that we view our lives through a set of lies
about ourselves, false stories of who we are and are meant to be,
never getting an accurate picture of ourselves. Through the
"lens" of the story of Jesus we are able to see ourselves truthfully
and call things by their proper names. Only through the story of
the cross of Christ do we see the utter depth and seriousness of
our sin. Only through this story that combines cross and resurrection do we see the utter resourcefulness and love of a God who
is determined to save sinners (Romans 3:21-25).

As Augustine noted, we are afflicted with restless hearts. We
want more. Yet our wants are unschooled, wide ranging, free
floating, ready to alight on the first sweet-smelling blossom that
comes our way. The problem, in the matter of desire, is not that
we deeply desire (in fact, apathy, *acedia*, may be a bigger modern
temptation than greed); we desire deeply the wrong things. We
attempt to assuage the longing in our restless hearts with that
which can never fully satisfy. Buddhism hopes to extinguish some
of this raging desire. Christianity hopes to enflame it and to
direct it toward its proper object.

We say, "I don't know much about fine food, but I know what I
like." Do we? We grab and consume, to a great degree, because we
do not really know what we want and so we grab everything in the
desperate fear that we might say no to the one thing that might
give our lives some meaning. Advertising feeds on this unfocused,
relentless desire, constantly augmenting the objects of our desire,
implying that consumption itself is a creative human act, regardless of the objects of our consumption. We exalt our "freedom of
choice" as the supreme mark of our freedom when, in our exercise

of this freedom, we look like slaves, jerked around by things because we have no means within us of wisely saying yes and no.

—⟨⟨⟩⟩— —⟨⟨⟩⟩— —⟨⟨⟩⟩— —⟨⟨⟩⟩— —⟨⟨⟩⟩—

St. Thomas Aquinas contended that the really sinful thing about sin is in the committing of the act, the doing of the sin. He knew that the Christian notion of Original Sin makes us thoroughly sinful beings rather than simply those incipiently good people who from time to time commit sinful acts. Aquinas notes that thoughts lead to acts and intentions are the prelude to action, so that, when you think about it, thinking is doing. Aquinas was attempting to stress that there is a big difference between thinking evil and actually doing it. Luther said much the same with his famous comment about our not being able to keep the birds from flitting around our heads, but having a duty to keep them from nesting in our hair. Who on earth would criticize us for merely *thinking* murderous thoughts, while successfully restraining ourselves from committing murder?

Jesus, that's who. The only time he outright said that somebody could send himself to hell, it was for speaking ill of one's neighbor. Jesus took away from his followers the perfectly natural, completely understandable, universal inclination to name our neighbor "thou fool!" (Edmund Burke said, in 1796, "All men that are ruined are ruined on the side of their natural propensities.") Why would Jesus not confine himself only to lustful action, rather than condemn the relatively harmless "lust of the heart"?

Here we come closer to an understanding of what makes sin, sin for Christians. For those of us who are trying to take Jesus seriously, sin is not a foible, a slipup; it is offense against and rebellion against our Creator. Sin is that which separates us from a holy and righteous God. Jesus makes the rather astounding claim that, when it comes to sin, it's the thought that counts. Sin not only hurts the neighbor who is sinned against but also reflexively bites the sinner too. Sin carries within itself its own punishment. It erodes the soul. It severs an intended relationship between Creator and creature. These sins are called sins because of the nature of God in Jesus Christ, not from some view of human nature.

I tend to think of temptation as a midlife-crisis sort of thing, something that hits you on a late afternoon in middle age. But the gospel here portrays encounters with the devil as happening early in one's career; at least it was that way for Jesus.

In the desert there are no clear paths, so you have to make your own way. Without city walls and civil protection, you are on your own in the desert. This is one reason why most of us fear being alone for too long, and why we must always have music pumping into our ears. Alone, in the quiet, in the desert, voices come, and for Jesus, the voice that comes, after the heavenly baptismal voice, is that of the devil.

"If you are the Son of God," (that is, if you are who the heavenly voice said you were at your baptism), "command this stone to become a loaf of bread." The person who could turn stones to bread could do a lot of good for poor, suffering humanity, and would be canonized quicker than Mother Teresa. Jesus says, "No."

True, says Satan, feed a man today; he'll only be hungry again tomorrow. Then, if you are the Son of God, do some good for the greatest number through the only long-term, effective means of doing good that we know—politics. Then Satan, in an instant, shows Jesus "all the kingdoms of the world" (4:5) and offers to hand them and all "their glory and all this authority" (4:6) to Jesus, "for it has been given to me, and I give it to anyone I please" (4:7), if Jesus will just worship the devil.

(Here we pause to wonder, who gave the devil all the nations of the world? Did God say, "Politics? I have no interest in such grubby affairs. Here, Satan, I'll let you have politics"? We don't know. All we know is that, when it comes to politics, there does seem to be an obvious linkage with worship of the devil.)

At any rate, Jesus again refuses. He even refuses religious, spiritual feats (4:9-11), refusing to throw himself down from the top of the temple and ask for angelic help, even though the baptismal voice said that he was the Son of God.

Note that the temptations of the devil are not just any old temptations. This is not about the piece of chocolate pie after dinner or the tempting sweet young thing in the negligee. This is a peculiar, specific temptation, vocational temptation. It's a debate between the devil and Jesus over who Jesus is. Each of the temptations is preceded by the devil's "If you are....then...." The baptismal voice has said, "This is my Son." If Jesus is indeed the very Son of God, so intimately connected with God, then he ought to act like God, or at least act like God would act if we were God—omnipotently. What is God if not unlimited, free, absolute power? And what is Pride but an exercise of, and a relishing in, our potency? This is what the serpent offered us, in offering us unlimited, unrestrained wisdom back in the Garden: "Your eyes will be opened, and you will be like God" (Genesis 3:5). Thus was the modern university founded.

And yet, Jesus says no.

Luke says that Satan sulked away, leaving Jesus "until an opportune time" (4:13). We hear no more of the devil or his temptations until the end of the Jesus story. As Jesus hangs on the cross in mortal agony, the devil's words are repeated nearly verbatim. The soldiers, those in the employ of the "kingdoms of this world," mock Jesus, saying, "If you are the King of the Jews, save yourself" (Luke 23:37). And the crowd (that's us) screams, "If you are the Messiah, save yourself and us" (23:39). Satan doesn't have to tempt Jesus this time. Now the devil's words are on our lips.

When Jesus was tempted in the desert, you will recall that the devil offered him only good things—bread, political power, and miraculous spiritual feats. Once you admit, and I think we must admit, to the goodness of material possessions, then greed is a very difficult line to draw.

But just because it is difficult, there is no reason why we should not draw such a line. Perhaps we ought to distinguish between what we need and what we want. We need many of the material possessions that we accumulate. We know of the necessity to "meet my needs." Yet how do you meet the ever-expanding reach of desire? Desire has a way of mimicking need. In the marketplace, advertising has a genius for performing that sleight-of-hand that moves us quickly from what we desire to what we need.

We live in a land ruled over by the Constitution that gives us all certain innate "rights." The purpose of this democracy is to give us our rights. Perhaps we are among the first generation in this society to realize that desire has a way of being elevated to the level of need, and need gets further inflated to the level of rights. Our rights are thus an ever-expanding list because my desires are a bottomless pit. Thus noble democracy becomes a relentless commercial supermarket where we rush about grabbing everything we can out of fear that we might neglect the one thing that would give us lives that are worth living.

Need is best if kept close to the basics—a full stomach, a roof over our heads. But it is the nature of desire to be ever growing, ever rising. And where do we get the wherewithal to say no? In our society—with the constant bombardment from advertising (Please, Lord, deliver me from unsolicited e-mail commercials), as well as all of the social affirmation of the "lifestyles of the rich and famous," whom no one dares to call merely Greedy—where might one get the moral stamina to say, "Enough is enough!"?

In one of the most notable and depressing failures in all of the Gospels, a rich man comes to Jesus asking, "Good teacher, what must I do to inherit eternal life?" (Luke 18:18), that is, what must I do to be saved? Jesus, who appears to have a low tolerance for rich, upwardly mobile, spiritual eager beavers at first brushes him off with, "Why do you call me good? Nobody is good but God." Not the most promising of beginnings for a thoughtful dialogue on religion.

Then Jesus merely repeats the demand that he obey all the commandments of God, perhaps thinking that will end the conversation. To Jesus' surprise, the man says that he has obeyed and never once broken all the commandments since he was a kid in Sabbath school. Who among us could say that?

Jesus, undeterred by the man's apparent spiritual success and lack of need (if he's that good, what on earth could Jesus add to his goodness?) thunders, "Go, sell all that you have and give it to the poor, then come, follow me." With that radical command to redistribute his wealth, the man slumped down and got depressed, muttering to himself, "I thought Jesus was a nice person." He climbs into his Porsche and departs.

Which leads Jesus to mutter, loud enough for all his disciples to hear, "You just can't save the rich people!" He compares the salvation of the rich to shoving a fully loaded dromedary through the narrow needle's eye. It's then that the disciples ask, "Who then can be saved?"

Lord, here's what we need today, right away, or as soon as we can get it: we need world peace, prosperity, security, life without risk, pleasure without pain, happiness without cost, and discipleship with no cross. That's why we're here, at church, to get our needs met. Our church tries to be user-friendly and seeker sensitive. That's why on Sundays we serve espresso with a dash of amaretto before our services, a little caffeine boost until we get to the main point of our worship: the prayer requests. So like we were saying, we need a quick recovery from gall bladder surgery, an effortless cataract removal, a happy marriage, obedient and chaste kids, and a reason to get out of bed in the morning. If you love us, you'll meet our needs.

Now then, is there something that we could do for you?

You're thirsty? Well, if you're the Messiah, why don't you fix yourself a divine drink? We've got needs of our own, thank you. It's our job to have need; it's your job to meet need.

For this and all other needs, spoken and unspoken, felt and unfelt, incipient and obvious, personal and corporate, immediate and long term, we pray. Amen.

I wonder if in our culture there is so much sexual passion and so little desire for God because sex has become the last means of self-transcendence. Sexual passion is our last means of getting outside ourselves, of having ourselves caught up in something greater than ourselves, our last momentary experience of mystery, our sole sacrament.

We ask of sex something that it can't deliver. I think of this often during a movie when the movie does a good job of getting some difficult, painful human problem out on the table for consideration—such as the life worth living, or the marriage worth having—and then ends in a romp between the sheets, as if sex were the cure for every ailment. What on earth does that have to do with anything? I ask myself at these movies. You may feel better for a moment, but you are still you, your life is unchanged, and you are still stuck where you were. Whoever said, "Love is the answer" could not have been talking about sexual love, which, no matter how momentarily good it gets, is not good enough fundamentally to change us. That's part of the fun of sex; it is so momentary, transitory, and fleeting. We thus confuse a temporary, momentary experience with a long-term solution, a short-lived experience of mystery with an experience of the true and living God, and that's the sin.

━◅◆▻━ ━◅◆▻━ ━◅◆▻━ ━◅◆▻━ ━◅◆▻━

I don't know what most impresses you about the story of the arrest, the trial, the crucifixion of Jesus. What impresses me is its sheer bloodiness, the violence. I pray to God that I'll never get so hardened of heart, so inoculated to the violence, that I cease to flinch as Jesus is nailed to the wood.

It's a very violent story. Jesus foretold this night in a parable (Matthew 21). A man had a vineyard. He improved it, built a wall around it, a tower too. He leased his vineyard to some tenants, allowing them to collect and keep the fruit of the vineyard, never charging them rent. One day, he sent his servants to the tenants to collect the rent that was due. The wicked tenants beat the servants, killing one, stoning another half to death. The owner thought, "Unbelievable! This time I'll send my own son to collect my rent. That will surely shame them, or bring out the best in them."

The owner failed fully to reckon the depth of wickedness, the potential for violence among the tenants. They said to themselves, "Well, here comes the son, the heir to the vineyard. Let's bash in his head, kill him, so that it will be ours." And Jesus says, the kingdom of God is just like that. He who never one time used violence or even self-defense (wouldn't let us use our swords tonight to protect him), was the cause of violence. He, who embodied the best, brought out in us the worst. The gospel is a violent story.

So is ours. We are a violent people, we tenants of the vineyard, and most of the stories about us, if they are true, are bathed in blood. Historian Stephen Ambrose says that 1945, the year before my birth, may have been history's bloodiest year. In every corner of the world, the sight, says Ambrose, of a half dozen teenaged boys, walking down a street, would strike fear among the people. They were armed to the teeth, young killers in uniforms provided by old men in government. I was born one year later, the year of the last lynching in the South, in my hometown. I was conceived in blood.

And weren't we all? Creation is but six chapters old, says Genesis (6:11), when God notes that something had gone terribly wrong. The earth that God intended to be filled with birds and beasts and humanity is "filled with violence."

And hasn't it always been that way, at least in our part of the earth? A three-volume book was published a few years ago entitled *Violence in America*. A brief perusal proves it really is as American as apple pie. We were born in blood, what we call "The Revolution" and others call the genocide of the natives. Consider: 168 people killed by a young man, U.S. Army–trained, in Oklahoma City. The crazed Unabomber, a Harvard man. Most of our children have seen about a thousand TV murders by the time they are ten. And so many of our heroes—Kennedy, King, Lincoln—assassinated by their fellow citizens. I confess I only made it through about twenty of the encyclopedia's nearly two thousand bloody pages.

And he gathered us, the night before he was whipped, beaten, and nailed to the wood. And taking the bread he said, "This is my body, broken, for you." And then the cup, "This is my blood, shed, for you." For you. Because if there were not some blood to it, some brokenness, it wouldn't be for me, for you.

A number of years ago I gave a series of lectures at a pastors' school on the West Coast. My subject: sin and its consequences. My remarks were not universally well received. A number in my audience—mostly men, middle aged, mainline Protestants— seemed rather baffled by my presentations, hurt even. After all, they seemed to say, we are educated, enlightened, socially progressive folk living in the Pacific Northwest who have over-come gloomy matters like sin that once were so overstressed by orthodox Christianity. Onward and upward, better and better every day in every way, that's our motto.

Among those who heard me gladly was a group of clergy-women. At first this surprised me. A number of feminist theolo-gians back then were quite critical of Augustinian preoccupation with sin, particularly the sin of pride, saying that such concern was oppressive to the full self-expression of women. But in talk-ing with these clergywomen about their experiences in the pas-toral ministry I realized a cold truth: if one is on top, well-fixed, secure, then one can afford to be sanguine about sin. People in power always think of ourselves as basically good people living in a well-ordered world. Why not? It is our world. To such folk, "prophetic ministry" means mostly minor tinkering with the present political structures, the passage of new legislation, help-ful advice to Congress. Our world, while needing certain modifi-cations, is basically good because it is our world.

But if one is on the bottom, at times victim of other people's cruelty and disregard, then one tends to have a different view of the world. As one of these clergywomen put it, "there is no way to explain how such nice people, the sort of people I have in my congregation, could be so mean—except that they are sinners." These women, having been called to ministry, were finding the church to be a risky place. The traditional Christian sense of sin made new sense to them. As Kierkegaard noted, "sin presupposes itself "into human endeavor, even (especially) endeavor that is ecclesiastical.

In his *People of the Lie,* Scott Peck says that if one is looking for genuine evil, then one ought to look first within the synagogue and church. It is of the nature of evil to "hide among the good." Satan masquerades as an angel of light. Lucifer is his name, after all. Leaders of the church beware, not only because we work among the godly, but also because we ourselves, called to speak to and for God to God's people, are in a morally vulnerable position where sin is always lurking about the door (Gen. 4:7).

I stand at the front door of the church. It is Sunday. I like to stand here and watch people entering the church. What unites them? Sinners come in the church. Some are still in their mother's arms. Sleeping, they come, but not of their own volition. They look innocent enough, but they are still sinners. Though outwardly cuddly and cute, they are among the most narcissistic and self-centered in the congregation. When they wake up, they will cry out, not caring that the rest of us are about important religious business. When they are hungry, they will demand to be fed, now. Cute, bundled up, placidly sleeping or peevishly screaming. Sinners. Sinners come to church. They are being led by the hand. They do not come willingly. Though they put up a fight an hour ago, a rule is a rule, and there they are. They have said that they hate church. They have said things about church that you wouldn't be allowed to have published in the local newspaper, if you were older. Ten years old they are, and they lack experience and expertise, but not in one area: they are sinners.

Sinners come in the church. Sullen, slouched, downcast eyes. They were out with friends last night to a late hour, and the incongruity between here in the morning and there last night is striking. They know it and it is only one of the reasons why they do not want to be here. Dirty thoughts. Desire. Things you are not supposed to think about. These thoughts make these sinners very uncomfortable at church.

Sinners come to church, and they have put on some weight, middle-aged, receding hairlines, "showing some age." They are holding on tight. Well-dressed, attempting to look very respectable, proper. Youthful indiscretions tucked away, put behind them, does anybody here know? A couple of things tucked away from the gaze of the IRS. And a night that wasn't supposed to happen two conventions ago. These sinners are looking over their shoulders. They are having trouble keeping things together. Maybe that is why there are so many of these sinners here, coming in the door of the church.

Sinners come in the church, and the doors at last are closed. The last of them scurry to their appointed seats. The organ music begins, played by an extremely talented, incredibly gifted artist, who is also a sinner. And the lyrics to that first hymn, something about "Amazing Grace," sung, appropriately, by those who really need it, need it in the worst way. They sing in the singular, but it ought to be in the plural. "Amazing grace that saved wretches like us."

Sinners come into church. And now for the chief of them all, the one most richly dressed, most covered up, the one who leads, and does most of the talking. Some call him pastor. Down deep, his primary designation is none other than that of those whom he serves. Sinners come into the church, and now their pastor welcomes them, their pastor, the one who on a regular basis presumes to speak up for God, making him the "chief of sinners."

Sinners come to church, all decked out, all dressed up, all clean and hopeful. Sinners, sinners hear the good news, "Christ Jesus came into the world to save sinners" (1 Timothy 1:15). Jesus called as his disciples Matthew, Mark, Luke, and John, Mary and Mary Magdalene. Sinners. Only sinners. And Jesus got into the worst sort of trouble for eating and drinking with sinners. Only sinners. Sinners.

Jesus saves sinners. Thank God. Only sinners. We sinners.

CHAPTER FIVE

GOOD NEWS

Cross

Really now, Lord Jesus, is our sin so serious as to necessitate the sort of ugly drama we are forced to behold this day? Why should the noon sky turn toward midnight and the earth heave and the heavens be rent for our mere peccadilloes? To be sure, we've made our mistakes. Things didn't turn out as we intended. There were unforeseen complications, factors beyond our control. But we meant well. We didn't intend for anyone to get hurt. We're only human, and is that so wrong?

Really now, Lamb of God who takes away the sins of the world, we may not be the very best people who ever lived, but surely we are not the worst. Others have committed more serious wrong. Ought we to be held responsible for the ignorance of our grandparents? They, like we, were doing the best they could, within the parameters of their time and place. We've always been forced to work with limited information. There's always been a huge gap between our intentions and our results.

Please, Lord Jesus, die for someone else, someone whose sin is more spectacular, more deserving of such supreme sacrifice. We don't want the responsibility. Really, Lord, is our unrighteousness so very serious? Are we such sinners that you should need to die for us?

Really, if you look at the larger picture, our sin, at least my sin, is so inconsequential. You are making too big a deal out of such meager rebellion. We don't want your blood on our hands. We don't want our lives in any way to bear the burden of your death. Really. Amen.

—⚬— —⚬— —⚬— —⚬— —⚬—

I was having a difficult time in my previous congregation. A stormy board meeting was followed by a poorly received sermon, which was then succeeded by a none-too-pleasant public confrontation with the chair of the church trustees. What had I done to so badly manage the congregation? I sat in my office, going over the events of the past week, attempting to take appropriate responsibility for the administrative mess I was in. Could I have been more discreet? Why had I felt the need to bring things to a head now? Had I abused the pulpit in last Sunday's sermon?

Then I returned to my preparation for next Sunday's sermon. Year B of the Common Lectionary, Mark. Another story of Jesus' teaching and healing. Another story of rejection. Then it hit me. Why was I so surprised that our congregation was full of conflict? Was the conflict a sign of my failure to skillfully manage congregational differences, or my skillful pastoral telling of the truth? I heard Mark ask, "What's the problem? You think that you are a better preacher than Jesus?"

> "If any want to become my followers, let them deny themselves and take up their cross and follow me. For those who want to save their life will lose it, and those who lose their life for my sake, and for the sake of the gospel, will save it." (Mark 8:34-35)

At that moment I recalled that just about 99 percent of Mark's Gospel encompasses the preparation to crucify Jesus, Jesus' crucifixion, or the aftermath of Jesus' crucifixion. The cross, it appears, is not optional equipment for a faithful ministry. The cross, the self-giving, emptying of God in the crucified Jesus—God's great victory over sin and death through divine suffering—is the primary ethical trajectory of the New Testament.

--------◆--------◆--------◆--------◆--------◆--------

Despite our earnest efforts, we couldn't climb all the way up to God. So what did God do? In an amazing act of condescension, on Good Friday, God climbed down to us, became one with us. The story of divine condescension begins on Christmas and ends on Good Friday. We thought, if there is to be business between us and God, we must somehow get up to God. Then God came down, down to the level of the cross, all the way down to the depths of hell. He who knew not sin took on our sin so that we might be free of it. God still stoops, in your life and mine, condescends.

"Are you able to drink the cup that I am to drink?" he asked his disciples, before his way up Golgotha. Our answer is an obvious, "No!" His cup is not only the cup of crucifixion and death, it is the bloody, bloody cup that one must drink if one is going to get mixed up in us. Any God who would wander into the human condition, any God who has this thirst to pursue us, had better not be too put off by pain, for that's the way we tend to treat our saviors. Any God who tries to love us had better be ready to die for it.

Earlier in this very same gospel, it was said, "The Word, the eternal Logos of God, became flesh and moved in with us, and we beheld his glory" (AP). Now the Word, the Christ of God, sees where so reckless a move ends: on a cross. "I thirst, I yearn to feast with you," he says, "and behold, if you dare, where it gets me."

When I was giving some lectures at a seminary in Sweden some years ago, a seminarian asked, "Do you really think Jesus Christ is the only way for us to get to God?"

And I thoughtfully replied, "I'll just say this, if you were born in South Carolina, and living in America, yes. There really is no way for somebody like me to get to God, other than a Savior who doesn't mind a little blood and gore, a bit of suffering and grizzly shock and awe, in order to get to me. A nice, balanced Savior couldn't do much for a guy like me. I need a fanatic like Jesus. For we have demonstrated that we are an awfully, fanatically cruel and bloody people when our security is threatened. We have this history of murdering our saviors. So I just can't imagine any other way to God except Jesus."

⬤⬤⬤⬤⬤

To tell the truth, Lord Jesus, we weren't that close to your cross when the soldiers nailed you to the wood and hoisted you up over Golgotha. But from where we were standing, at a safe distance, it looked to us like your arms were extended just about as far as they could go. It made us very uncomfortable to see your arms stretched out so very wide.

Yet you tended to do that, even before you got your cross. Seeing you hanging there, arms in such unnatural embrace, we recalled how troublesome was your reach throughout your ministry, a real pain. First the dirty, common fisherfolk whom you called to abandon their families and follow you, then the tax collectors, the whores, the lepers, the stumbling blind and crawling lame, cruel Roman soldiers, bleeding women, clergy, even corpses, all responding to your touch, all caught within your grasp. A Savior can't reach that far and not expect to be punished for it. And on Friday, God knows you paid dearly for your barrier-breaking, boundary-bursting reach.

You overreached.

How wide is your reach? See, even now, the nails through your hands cannot constrain you. You stoop, strain, bend, and grab, reaching down all the way to hell itself, determined to gather, to reap, to have all us sinners, dead or alive, no matter what the sin, all in your clutch, all in your embrace.

We gather here, at the foot of your cross as those who have been grabbed, got hold of, by a Lord whose reach knows no bounds. So this day, this fateful Friday, we warn those not yet reached—Hitler, Stalin, the woman sitting next to us today on the bus, the man who yesterday cut us off in traffic and grinned about it, the one who so wronged me that I hate him and wish he were not, the Palestinian who strapped the plastic explosive to herself and pulled the cord hoping to take some Jewish children with her—beware. Take it from us sinners: His reach is without bounds, His embrace wide, determined and irresistible. He will have you, if He has to die trying. Amen.

Don't you find it curious that the first word, the very first word that Jesus speaks in agony on the cross, is "Father, forgive"? Such blood, violence, injustice, crushed bone, and ripped sinew, the hands nailed to the wood. With all the possible words of recrimination, condemnation, and accusation, the first thing Jesus says is, "Father, forgive." Earlier he commanded us to forgive our enemies and to pray for those who persecute us. We thought he meant that as a metaphor. (I can't tell you how long it's been since I've uttered a really good prayer for the souls of Saddam Hussein or Osama bin Laden.) On the cross, Jesus dares to pray for his worst enemies, the main foes of his good news, us.

How curious of Jesus to unite ignorance and forgiveness. I usually think of ignorance as the enemy of forgiveness. I say, "Forgiveness is fine—as long as the perpetrator first knows and then admits that what he did was wrong." First, sorrowful, knowledgeable repentance, then secondary, gracious forgiveness. Right?

Yet here, from the cross, is preemptive forgiveness. We begin with forgiveness. Jesus' first word is forgiveness. It's as if, when God the Father began creating the world, the first word was not "Let there be light" but rather "Let there be forgiveness." There will be no new world, no order out of chaos, no life from death, no new liaison between us and God without forgiveness first.

Forgiveness is the first step, the bridge toward us that only God can build. The first word into our darkness is, "Father, forgive."

"Father, forgive," must always be the first word between us and God, because of our sin and because of God's eternal quest to have us. Forgiveness is what it costs God to be with people like us who, every time God reaches out to us in love, beat God away. Here on the cross, God the Father had two possibilities, the way I see it. One, God could abandon us. God could have said, "All right, that's enough. I did everything possible to reach toward them, embrace them, save them, bring them toward myself, but when they stooped to killing my Son, that's it." God could have abandoned us at this moment. Or, two, God the Father could have abandoned God the Son, handed him over into our sinful hands. God could have left the Son to hang there as the hapless, helpless victim of our evil.

But these were never real options for God if God were to continue to be the God who is revealed to us in Scripture. God the Father cannot be separated from God the Son. God the Father stays with the Son and in the suffering and horror gets us in the bargain. God the Father stays with us and gets a crucified Son. The unity of the Trinity is maintained—Father, Son, and Holy Spirit—and in so doing, the Father and the Holy Spirit take on the suffering of the Son. The Father of course could not have abandoned the Son without abandoning who the Father really is. So the Father maintains the life of the Trinity by uniting with us through massive forgiveness, for there is no way for God the Father and God the Holy Spirit to be with God the Son, the Incarnate Word, without being with us murderers of God.

Here, at the cross, we are now not splashing about in the shallow end of the pool. Here, even the most complacent minds realize that Jesus has led us into deep waters. Here, religion is significantly more than something "spiritual," more than an uplifting thought or noble idea that we can all sit around and discuss and then go home and forget. Here religion has somehow taken hold of our whole being, consumed us, knocked us off balance, and demanded our last anguished breath. Jesus says, "I thirst."

There is a parched desiccation within us that will only be assuaged by God, by the living God. In his deep anguish, in his thirsting, they offered him a sponge with vinegar on a stick. But Jesus was thirsty for more than water. Jesus had a deep, blessed thirst that God's will be done on earth as in heaven, that God's righteousness might be fulfilled to the brim, a holy thirst that could only be assuaged, by lifting up the blood-red cup of salvation and drinking it to the dregs.

But maybe Jesus isn't talking about *our* thirst or *our* hunger. He says "I" thirst. Not you, not me. He said, "I thirst." God Almighty, the Son of the Father is thirsty. The mocking soldiers offered him a sponge soaked in vinegar just to scorn him in his thirst.

But maybe he wasn't thirsty even for water. Maybe he was thirsty for his righteousness' sake. Maybe he was thirsty for us. Is not that a fair summary of much of Scripture—God's got this thing for us? God is determined—through Creation, the words of the prophets, the teaching of the law, the birth of the Christ—to get close to us. God has this unquenchable thirst to have us. Even us.

⸺ ⸺ ⸺ ⸺ ⸺

How did he say "It is finished"? I think he said it not in defeat—I've done the best I could, now I give up, give in, and die—but in victory—I've fought the fight, faced Satan down, and now my work is stunningly accomplished. The scapegoat who took on the sins of Israel, driven out into the wilderness to die, has now become the Lamb of God who, driven back to the throne of God, atones for the sins of the whole world.

As Paul says, the only righteous One who knew no sin was made to bear all our sin that we sinners might become the righteous of

God (1 Cor. 1:30). Don't ask me to explain that thick thought. You are not meant to figure it out, just sit there this day and behold it.

As we once said in the old Communion prayer, "he offered there for us a full, sufficient, and perfect sacrifice for the sins of the whole world." God has now finished the work that God began with us so long ago. God was determined, having created us, having loved us in so many and diverse ways, to get back to us. And now God has. It is finished.

Listen to this, oh ye purpose-driven, upwardly mobile, goal-setting high achievers. He has done what we could not do. Because we could not get up to God, God climbed down to us, got down on our level, and here, in the bloody, unjust crucifixion, we have at last descended to our level. God has finished what God began. It is finished.

What now is to be done by us? Nothing.

What might we learn from the lessons of this day? Nothing.

What are we supposed to do for God before nightfall? Nothing. Did you miss his words? "It is finished."

Resurrection

A student, asked to summarize the gospel in a few words, responded: in the Bible, it gets dark, then it gets very, very dark, then Jesus shows up. I'd add to this affirmation, Jesus doesn't just show up; he shows up *for us*.

As the psalmist declared:

> Where can I go from your spirit?
>   Or where can I flee from your presence?
> If ascend to heaven, you are there;
>   if I make my bed in Sheol, you are there. (Ps 139:7-8)

I was visiting a man as he lay dying, his death only a couple of days away. I asked him there at the end what he was feeling. Was he fearful?

"Fear? No," he responded, "I'm not fearful because of my faith in Jesus."

"We all have hope that our future is in God's hands," I said, somewhat piously.

"Well, I'm not hopeful because of what I believe about the future," he corrected me, "I'm hopeful because of what I've experienced in the past."

I asked him to say more.

"I look back over my life, all the mistakes I've made, all the times I've turned away from Jesus, gone my own way, strayed, and got lost. And time and again, he found a way to get to me, showed up and got me, looked for me when I wasn't looking for him. I don't think he'll let something like my dying defeat his love for me."

There was a man who understood Easter.

To the poor, struggling Corinthians, failing at being the church, backsliding, wandering, split apart, faithless, scandalously immoral, Paul preaches Easter. He reminds them that they are here, *ekklesia,* gathered and summoned by the return of the risen Christ. Earlier, God declared, "I will be their God and they will be my people." That's the story that, by the sheer grace of God, continues. That's what this risen Savior does. He comes back—again and again—to the very ones (I'm talking about us!) who so betray and disappoint him. He appears to us, seeks us, finds, grabs us, embraces, holds on to us, commissions us to do his work. In returning to his disciples, the risen Christ makes each of us agents of Easter. "As the Father has sent me," Jesus says, "so I send you" (John 20:21).

⊸⊸⊸ ⊸⊸⊸ ⊸⊸⊸ ⊸⊸⊸ ⊸⊸⊸

Sometimes people say, "God? Oh, can't say anything definitive about God. God is large, nebulous, and vague." We wish. By rendering God into an abstract idea, we can be assured that we'll always be safe from God. By raising the crucified Jesus from the dead, it was as if God vindicated Jesus, as if God said, "You want to know what God looks like? You want to know what the Creator really wants from the creature and creation? Look at Jesus! There, that's who I am." At a definite point in time, at a particular place, in love, God allowed God's self to be pinned down by us—on a cross. It's a curious thing to say about Jesus, the wandering teacher of Galilee, that he is as much of God as we ever hope to see. Even more so, Jesus is a curious thing to say about God.

It wasn't simply that, "God has raised a person from the dead." Who would have gotten worked up over, "God has raised Julius Caesar from the dead"? Rather, the Christian message was, "God raised *Jesus* from the dead." God raised this one who forgave his enemies, who reached out to the sinner and the outcast, who stood up to the authorities, and who invited everyone to his kingdom. That One is raised.

The Greeks tried to overcome time through imagining divinity as that which lacks all temporal boundaries. Greek gods transcend death by their immunity to the ravages of time. Christians see things differently. The triune God transcends death by triumphing over it, by the Son's dying in time and by the Father's raising him up in the power of the Holy Spirit for all time. The Greeks saw divinities as serene, ideal, and only occasionally, capriciously descending from Parnassus to become briefly involved in the grubby vicissitudes of human history. The resurrection narratives depict a God who is constantly on the move, energetic, revealing here, now. The Greeks predicated a quiet serenity at the ultimate heart of all things. Easter stories depict a God who refuses to stop talking and cease walking. Here is a God who takes time, not to be immune from time's vicissitudes, but to be eternally faithful in time. "Your faithfulness endures to all generations . . ." (Ps 119:90). In every generation God keeps rising up and defeating time in order to keep God's commitments in time, in order to keep talking, keep relating. Thus Easter brings us to the heart of Christian preaching and life with a God in time who refuses to be silent. The Easter mandate is the vocative, "Go! Tell!"

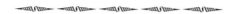

When we die, we die. We don't just appear to be snuffed out, then to sail forth into some vague metaphysical, shadowy state. We return to the dust from which we came. Tears and wailing are appropriate responses from loved ones when the sting of death strikes their beloved. And yet, in a spectacular miracle of God, the same God who raised dead Jesus somehow reaches in, defeats the enemy death, and takes us along as well. Jesus was resurrected into some new "body" whereby he appeared to his disciples in his resurrected state. It was a very different body—he could walk through doors, appear and disappear to his disciples. They did not readily recognize him in his resurrected body but still, after a few bodily acts—like touching him and eating with him—they recognized him as the same Jesus whom they loved, followed, and at times disobeyed, although he was Jesus in a wonderfully different form. Yet there is even more. The bold claim of his disciples was not only that Jesus was raised, but he promised to reach in and resurrect them as well. "Because I live," said Jesus, "you'll live too." So John Calvin spoke of our reconciliation to God as "vivification," restored to God, we are vivified.

Immortality is attractive because it acts as if eternality is something that we possess as human beings. Resurrection is humbling because it is pure gift to utterly mortal beings like us. Immortality usually assumes continuity in the next life with this life—if we enjoyed rose gardening in this life, we'll get to garden in the next.

Resurrection promises a whole new world, a radical discontinuity with the pain and frustration of life in this world, discontinuity that occurs because we are now near God in a healed, restored, wonderfully refashioned world.

⚞⚟ ⚞⚟ ⚞⚟ ⚞⚟ ⚞⚟

Listen to most Easter hymns and many Easter sermons and you might think that the whole point of Easter is, "Jesus is raised … and now we too shall get to go to heaven," with the emphasis decidedly on the second half of that affirmation. This is a strange take on Easter when one considers that the gospel resurrection narratives seem unconcerned about our future hope. Paul drew out a future hope for us as an implication of Jesus' resurrection, but that does not appear to be a first-order interest in Paul and certainly is not an explicit concern of the synoptic Gospels. In a sense, the risen Christ is not so much the one who rescues us now from having one day forever to die but rather he rescues us today from having to live with no hope beyond America.

I've just finished teaching an undergraduate course on Jesus. As part of the course we viewed a number of films on Jesus (including *Jesus of Montreal* and *The Last Temptation of Christ*). The students noted that most of these films have a gritty, first-century, Near Eastern verisimilitude about them—you really believe that you are there. Until they get to the resurrection. At the resurrection the camera becomes unfocused, everything gets fuzzy, blurred, and pastel.

How different from the Gospel narratives of Easter. The Gospels give the story of Easter an utterly this-world, present-age significance. Jesus Christ—whom we crucified—is revealed in his resurrection to be the true Lord of the world, this world, not some future world. Jesus is raised to reign now, not later. Thus the Easter narratives are accounts of vocation. Witnesses of the resurrection have a job to do—to tell the whole world the truth that

Jesus Christ is Lord and all other presumed lordlets are not. "Go...tell!"

It is as if the Gospel accounts of Easter try not to give encouragement to those who attempt to make Jesus' resurrection an otherworldly, spiritual experience. The Gospels present the resurrection of Jesus as a political event, that which happens here, now in the Gospel mix of fear, misapprehension, evening meals, locked doors, breakfast on the beach, and the disciples' sexist unwillingness to believe the testimony of women. God's new age has broken into the present time, our time. And the first to get the news were not good, spiritually perceptive people; they were people like us. We do not live in a perpetual state of pious Eucharistic adoration; our world is the dreary world of breakfast, soggy cornflakes, doubt, and fear. We gather, in your church and mine, not with spiritually perceptive, fully believing, undoubting Christians; we gather with those who, when it comes to Jesus' resurrection, are convinced that Caesar calls the shots. We are as clueless as Simon Peter, shocked and utterly unprepared that the risen Christ should appear to a loser like him.

We believe that the limits of our lives—the *boundedness* of life as fixed by God—is also a gracious gift of God. Our time is restricted. This life is not fated to go on forever, one damned thing, or one blessed thing, after another. Our lives are bounded not just by death but by Providence, Presence.

How can such knowledge—our time is finite, bounded in death—be considered a gracious gift? This is an insight granted to those who know that our lives are bounded *by God*. Death is the great boundary of life and, in the resurrection of Jesus Christ, God is the great boundary of death. Death limits life, but on Easter God limited death. Only then death loses its quality as the great final fact, the dominator of every moment of life. In Easter, death stops seeming like judgment, a curse, the thief, the final enemy, and begins to appear as forgiveness, blessing, sometimes even friend. No stoic resignation, the stiff upper lip of the doomed, is now demanded. Rather, thanksgiving, rejoicing even, which is what Revelation says our future is like. The door that was shut to us in death swings open, not by our striving or our positive attitude but rather by God. That which heretofore was exclusively ending is—surprise—beginning. We are not just given more time (in my pastoral experience, few people who are near death want that). We are given more radiant time, more presence time, time more fully to be with God and God with us.

God not only takes time, but God gives us time. We genuinely do have time. We have a present and a future because God gives it to us. When I take time to give someone else an hour of my time, that is one of my greatest gifts. I am literally giving them time, transforming their time by my willingness to enter their time and to allow them to enter mine.

Christians believe that something like that has happened in Jesus Christ.

What does it take to see? It is not enough to say, "Well, what you see is what you get." There is this matter of failed vision, inadequate perception. We've all had that frustrating experience of seeing something at some distant point across the landscape. And then we say to the friend beside us, gesturing, "Look, over there!"

What enables us to see? What grabs our gaze, turns our eyes in the right direction, and brings all into focus?

For Mary and for Thomas, it was the Risen Christ. Jesus not only rose from the dead, but appeared to the very ones who had forsaken him. He did not leave them to their own devices or their misperceptions. He came to them. He spoke to one, calling her by name; he encouraged the other to touch his very body. He turned their gaze away from that which was expected and accustomed toward that which was revealed.

Maybe that is why we call Christianity a "revealed religion." You can't "see it" until it is shown you. You are given the gift of the presence of the Risen Christ, and then you see and then you believe.

What if seeing, real seeing, is not an intellectual achievement of hard work and a good epistemological method, but a gift? You see, I think the story of Mary at the tomb, and Thomas in doubt, is a story about you. You got Easter the same way they got Easter. You are here, not because you did an analysis of various Near Eastern immortality myths and concluded that the resurrection of Jesus made sense. You are here because the Risen Christ, in some way or another, called your name. "Mary." "George." "Courtney." And hearing your life addressed, you saw.

Others of you are the Thomas type. You are not good with abstractions. You need visible, tangible proof. One of you told me that you drove three hours this morning, arising at daybreak to be here for the service in Duke Chapel. When I said that I—having seen a preview of the sermon—thought it not worth such a drive, you said, "I'm not coming for the sermon. I'm coming for the building, the music, the bells." You explained, "I'm not that great a believer. Never have been. Can't get all those fancy theological ideas. I need something large and tangible if I'm to believe."

I think you had been reading the twentieth chapter of John's Gospel. Seeing really is believing. Most of the time we "see through a mirror dimly," as Paul put it. We're in the dark. Occasionally, by the grace of God, things come into focus and we see. We see, not as an intellectual achievement on our part, but as a gift on God's part. The Risen Christ loves us enough to give us what we need to see and to believe—our name called in the darkness, his body and blood given into our probing fingers. John's Gospel ends with John saying, "I wrote this gospel down in order that you might believe." The Risen Christ gives us what we need.

A few years ago a young man came to me complaining that he was "losing my faith." He had real problems with the virginal conception of Jesus, with the miracles, with resurrection. I talked with him, reasoned with him, argued with him, I suggested a book he might read: I remember it as a frustrating conversation. I hadn't seen him since his graduation from Duke until, this past January, preaching up at Harvard, he greeted meat the door of Memorial Chuch, just as bursting with belief as he could be. What happened? I told him I recalled that afternoon we discussed his faith.

He had no recollection of ever having had a conversation with me.

I won't bore you with the details, but he said there had been a series of interesting events, a voice in the night, coincidences, In short, he had been addressed, encountered. Now, he was home. He believed on the basis of having his name called.

It would have been news enough that Christ had died, but the good news was that he died *for us*. As Paul said elsewhere (Romans 5), one of us might be willing to die for a really good person, but Christ shows that he is not one of us by his willingness to die for sinners like us. His response to our sinful antics was not to punish or judge us. Rather, he came back to us, flooding our flat world not with the wrath that we deserved but with his vivid presence that we did not deserve.

It would have been news enough that Christ rose from the dead, but the good news was that he rose *for us*.

That first Easter, nobody actually saw Jesus rise from the dead. They saw him afterwards. They didn't appear to him; he appeared to them. Us. In the Bible, the "proof " of the resurrection is not the absence of Jesus' body from the tomb; it's the presence of

Jesus to his followers. The gospel message of the resurrection is not first, "Though we die, we shall one day return to life," it is, "Though we were dead, Jesus returned *to us*." If it was difficult to believe that Jesus was raised from the dead, it must have been almost impossible to believe that he was raised and returned to us. The result of Easter, the product of the resurrection of Christ is the church—a community of people with nothing more to convene us than that the risen Christ came back to us. That's our only claim, our only hope. He came back to Galilee. He came back to us.

I visit churches where they have a "Seeker Service" on Sunday mornings. Sometimes they have a "Seeker Service" on Saturday night. What's a "Seeker Service"? It's worship trimmed to the limitations of those who don't know much about church, where the music is all singable, and all the ideas are understandable, and the preachers are adorable. It's designed for people who are "seeking" something better in their lives.

Of course the church should reach out to people, including those who seek something better in their lives. Trouble is that's not the way the Bible depicts us. Scripture is not a story about how we kept seeking God. As we demonstrated on Good Friday and Holy Saturday, we can adjust to death. We can get along just fine without Jesus. So back to work, back to what we were doing before Jesus called us, back to Galilee. Nobody expected, even less wanted a resurrection.

But on Easter we were encountered by a Christ who was unwilling to let the story of us and God end in death. Easter is the story about how God keeps—despite us—seeking us.

On Easter, and in the days afterward, the risen Christ showed up among us while we were back at work out in Galilee—when he "appeared to Cephas, then to the twelve. Then he appeared to more than five hundred brothers and sisters at one time, . . . Then he appeared to James, then to all the apostles. Last of all, . . . he appeared also" to the great persecutor and murderer of the church named Paul. The risen Christ was only doing what the crucified Jesus always did: *he came back to us.*

━━◁◁◁Ⅱ▷▷▷━ ━◁◁◁Ⅱ▷▷▷━ ━◁◁◁Ⅱ▷▷▷━ ━◁◁◁Ⅱ▷▷▷━ ━◁◁◁Ⅱ▷▷▷━

Paul was stunned by the reality of the resurrection—the way God not only vindicated Jesus by raising him from the dead, but also thereby recreated the whole *kosmos.* In Easter, an old world had terminated and a new one was being born, so Paul was forced to rethink everything that he had previously thought, including ethics. Much of what Paul says about Christian behavior was formed as his testimony to the resurrection, an event that he had experienced within the dramatic turnaround in his own life. Yet there was nothing merely subjective in Paul's vocation. The call of Paul the apostle was his experience of finding himself living in a whole new world. He changed because of his realization that, in Jesus Christ, the world had changed. Paul's key testimonial to this recreation is in his Second Letter to the Corinthians:

> So if anyone is in Christ, there is a new creation: everything old has passed away; see, everything has become new! All this is from God, who reconciled us to himself through Christ, and has given us the ministry of reconciliation. (2 Cor. 5:17-18)

Verse 17, in the Greek, lacks both subject and verb so it is best rendered by the exclamatory, "If anyone is in Christ—new creation!"

Certainly, old habits die hard. There are still, as Paul acknowledges so eloquently in Romans 8, "the sufferings of this present time" (v. 18). The resistance and outright rejection that many women pastors suffer are evidence that the church has not yet fully appreciated the eschatological, end-of-the-age, transformed social arrangements that ought to characterize the church. That many ministers base their ministry on models of leadership uncritically borrowed from the latest fads in business or other secular leadership practices is yet another testimony to our failure to

88

believe that God raised Jesus Christ from the dead, thus radically changing everything. It makes a world of difference whether or not one knows about the resurrection. Thus, making doxology to God (Rom. 11:33-36), Paul asks that we present ourselves as "a living sacrifice, holy and acceptable to God" by not being "conformed to this world" but by being "transformed by the renewing of your minds" (Rom. 12:1-2). All of this is resurrection talk, the sort of tensive situation of those who find their lives still in an old, dying world, yet who also are conscious of a new world being born. Our lives are eschatologically stretched between the sneak preview of the new world being born among us in the church and the old world where the principalities and powers are reluctant to give way. In the meantime, which is the only time the church has ever known, we live as those who know something about the fate of the world that the world does not yet know.

How can one read the resurrection narratives without being impressed by their humor? Among the most astounded and disbelieving of the resurrection are Jesus' own disciples. Even when the risen Christ takes time to explain everything to them, they fail to get it (Luke 24:13-27). I love John's laconic comment that, after witnessing the spectacular first Easter, the empty tomb and all, "Then the disciples returned to their homes" (John 20:10). They went home! These were the sort of folk who could witness a resurrection and then go back to business as usual. If an early church father's characterization of Easter as "the joke that God played on the Devil" is true, then most of his disciples, at least at the first, did not get the joke. In a way, Easter keeps on being God's great joke played on the despair and the prudence of a church more willing to believe in Good Friday than in Easter.

Jesus is accosted by a church official who pleads, "My daughter's dying." Jesus and the official, Jarius, go home together. On the way a woman, who has been hemorrhaging for twelve years, who has used up her life savings on medical bills and ineffective therapies, pushes through the crowd and touches Jesus. We don't know her name. She is introduced as a woman who is sick and has suffered much at the hands of doctors. Her sickness has named her, dominated her, consumed her, which is what dying tends to do.

"If I could just touch him, I'd be healed," she says. She would have an identity other than her sickness.

And she is healed. This woman, enslaved by sickness for over a decade, as good as dead, named by her dying, is healed, brought back from the dead. We don't know what theology she adhered to, or if she was active in the Synagogue. All we know is that she reached out, touched Jesus, and received resurrection, just by touching him.

Now this healing-on-the-way is wonderful but by the time Jesus gets to Jairus' house, it's all over. His beloved little girl is dead. The weeping and wailing tell the sad news. Unfortunately Jesus has come too late to help the little girl.

"Why are you making such a fuss?" Jesus asks. "Mr. Lord of Life is here!" And the crowd turns from tears and mourning to mocking laughter. "Sure, like she's only asleep!" Nice timing, Jesus. You're late.

And Jesus touches her, announces, "It's time to get up!" And the derisive laughter becomes shocked wonder. Jesus' disciples, the ones gathered in this house of death, were "astounded." And even though it's not Easter, even though it's the dead of summer, whenever Jesus shows up, it's Easter. They were astounded.

We still are.

Here is the church, the insiders, us, all adjusted to death. Stoic resignation is about the best our theology can deliver. Mainline, Protestant Christians, in our membership malaise, console ourselves with, "Everybody's losing members." Amen. Decline is prevalent. Amen. Death is normal, we say with a knowing smirk. Declining birthrates among liberal, mainline Protestants lead to declining congregations. Simple as that. Church growth? It's a gimmick, a simplistic quick fix best suited for less progressive and well-educated congregations, we say with a progressive sneer.

"Do you think my son will ever get over his drug addiction?" she asked me. And I, as her enlightened pastor, replied, in love, "Recovery from heroin? What are the chances of that? Get serious. Get real." Mocking laughter is the way a sophisticated, stoic disposition refers to talk of Easter.

That expression, "Get real," translated into today's Scripture means "adjust to death." So when this desperate father presses in upon Jesus, when this poor, harried woman reaches toward Jesus, the home folks react with a sardonic smile. Jesus responds by offering some sufferers new life, hope, a future. Jesus doesn't say some magical incantation, doesn't offer some esoteric technique. Jesus just shows up. He allows the woman just to touch him. He speaks to the dead girl. And there is resurrection.

⊷⊶ ⊷⊶ ⊷⊶ ⊷⊶ ⊷⊶

"Lazarus, whom you love is ill, come quickly," entreated Jesus' good friends, Mary and Martha, Lazarus' sisters who lived in Bethany. Oddly, Jesus lingered where he was for three more days. What was he doing that was so important? John just says that Jesus hung out where he was for "three more days."

Of course, when Jesus finally shows up in Bethany three days later, it was all over but the weeping; Lazarus had been entombed for three days. Martha gave Jesus a piece of her mind for his malingering. If Jesus loved Lazarus so much, why did it take him so long to get there? He must have loved something else even more.

Upon hearing that Lazarus was dead, John says, "Jesus wept."

It's a comfort that Jesus feels our pain, his humanity connecting with ours. Then Jesus said something strange: "I am the resurrection and the life." He didn't say that he has come to tell grieving Martha about the resurrection. He didn't say, "Martha, take heart, one day, someday, your brother will be resurrected, and then you'll get to see him again in heaven." Jesus never talked like that.

Rather, Jesus says, "*I* am the resurrection and the life." Wherever I am, even here at this time and place of death, there is resurrection, and there is life, here, now. With that, Jesus acts on his compassion, goes out to the cemetery and, in a voice loud enough to wake the dead, shouts, "Lazarus, arise!" Lazarus comes forth like a mummy. "Unbind him!" Next thing you know, there's Jesus with Lazarus and his sisters, having a party in Bethany, and Jesus' critics (ever the guardians of the status quo) were planning now to kill him.

Why would you want to kill Jesus for resuscitating a dead man? I'll explain: The authorities had a monopoly on who gets life and who doesn't. They couldn't have some uneducated conjurer running around loose, implying that there's a power available that's as strong as the American Medical Association.

This story is a parable. The church always reads this story on a Sunday in Lent, season of the cross, as a kind of preview of Easter. Even though it's not yet Easter, whenever Jesus, Mr. Resurrection and the Life, shows up at the cemetery, corpses rise, the dead walk, things are cut loose, and the clergy get nervous.

Salvation

Like most of Scripture, the story of the man in the ditch is a story about God before it is a story about us, about the oddness of our salvation in Christ. I've used this interpretation of the parable of the good Samaritan before, and I can tell you that my congregation didn't like it. They like stories about themselves more than they like to hear stories about God. They are resourceful, educated, gifted people who don't like to be cast in the role of the beaten poor man in the ditch. They would rather be the anything-but-poor Samaritan who does something nice for the less fortunate among us. In other words, they don't like to admit that just possibly they may need to be saved.

Why is this story not about us? Doesn't the story end with Jesus saying to his interrogator, "Go and do likewise"? "Go" and "do" what? I'm saying that more difficult even than reaching out to the victim in the ditch (which is hard enough for us) is coming to conceive of yourself as the victim, learning to live as if your one last hope is the Savior whom you tend to despise.

The Samaritan is more than a moralistic story about how we ought to do good for others but rather a joke about how Jesus makes all of us look poor and beaten up and then teaches us to receive the God we've got. When Jesus was criticized for the company he kept at table, he was clear that he saves only the abandoned and the dying (Luke 19:10). But that also means that we can expect some resistance to the notion that Jesus Christ is *our* salvation. In John's Gospel we looked upon Immanuel, God with us, and cried, "you are a Samaritan and have a demon" (John 8:48). Many looked upon God's salvation—a Jew from Nazareth who lived briefly, died violently, and rose unexpectedly—and responded, "We would rather die in the ditch than to be saved by you." Therefore, the story of our salvation is, at key points, a story of our resistance, our violence to the Savior we did not expect.

Jesus reacts to our situation in the ditch, not with more rules and regulations, not with harsh condemnation, but with a sort of love that can only be called reckless, extravagant, prodigal. There is, dare I say it, a kind of promiscuous quality in his extroverted love.

To be loved by *this* person can be a challenge. The most controverted, tensive, and challenging thing about salvation in Jesus Christ is that it is *salvation in Jesus Christ.* If there is "no other name . . . by which we must be saved" (Acts 4:12), then those of us who know Jesus ought to understand better than anyone why many resist his rescue.

The popular movie *Crash* opens with a disgusting scene as an African American couple is stopped by two Caucasian policemen. One of the policemen, an obviously troubled middle-aged man, humiliates the couple by touching and probing the woman on the pretense that he is doing a search of her body, looking for weapons. It is a humiliating experience of racism and sexist evil. The couple is enraged but feels helpless to do anything about it. Eventually, they separate, so angry is the woman that her husband stood by and did nothing, so humiliated and angry is the man that he was a helpless bystander as his beloved was humiliated by this racist cop.

Later in the movie, the same policeman comes upon a terrible accident. A car has flipped upside down. It is leaking gas. Trapped inside is the driver. The policeman moves into action, crawling inside the car. But when he climbs inside and the trapped driver sees him, she begins screaming, "No, no! Not you. Get away from me. Don't touch me!"

It is the same woman whom he earlier humiliated. She is obviously terrified to see him. Though she hangs upside down, and though gasoline is leaking all around her, she can't stand the thought of being near this man again, much less having him save her.

But the policeman acts as he has been trained. He attempts to calm her. He tells her that she is going to make it. He pulls out his knife and cuts her free, gently letting her down in the upside down car, eventually pulling her to safety just before the car explodes in flames.

As she is led away by others, she looks over her shoulder and sees that the cop, the man who had so terribly wronged her now is the one responsible for saving her life. She must live as one who has been saved, indebted to a man whom she hates. Her savior is the perpetrator of a terrible, sinful act. It is all very complicated.

Salvation is complicated because of the complicated trinitarian God who saves. We are saved by the one whom we despise. Unlike in *Crash*, we are saved not by the one who abused us, but the one whom we abused. The one whom we crucified in a desperate attempt to be left alone becomes our savior who refuses to be God without us. And in being saved we are also indebted, enlisted, and bound in discipleship to the one who has suffered because of us and yet suffered for us in order to save us. Our salvation by the crucified Christ thus presses upon us heavy responsibility to live with the risen Christ. His salvation makes our lives more complex than if we had not been reached to and embraced by him. Even now God is searching through the large collection of divine fishhooks for just the right lure to catch you in order to embrace you in order eternally to enjoy you.

At certain key moments, Scripture is thus a kind of dialogue, not by equal partners, but still a dialogue that is God's grace. We must therefore be suspicious of abstract, impersonal, generic notions of God that make abstract claims that God is omnipotent, utterly free, and transcendent. Abstractions mean nothing apart from the specific narratives of Scripture that tell us what true power, freedom, and transcendence look like now that God looks like a crucified and resurrected Jew from Nazareth. God is the loving Father, Son, and Holy Spirit whose great sovereignty is that self-elected freedom to be in conversation, even free to be dissuaded by the pleas of someone like Moses, in order to be who God really is—God *pro nobis*.

When Christians say that God is "transcendent," this is what we are trying to say. The hiddenness and distance of God are precisely in God's nearby self-revelation as God on the cross. God's difference from our expectations for gods makes God hidden to us. We are resistant to the near God on the cross because of our assumption that if there were a true God, that God would be somewhere a long way from us, not here before us, naked, exposed and bleeding, certainly not one with us, not *pro nobis*. A righteous God would be aloof from us sinners, certainly not intrude through our locked doors (John 20) to show us his hands full of holes and to make us touch the gash in his side, to breathe his Holy Spirit upon us and thereby make his betrayers also his Body, his church, this God resurrected *pro nobis*.

Scripture's curious story of salvation is the story of a God who makes a world and delightedly calls it "good," though the Creation gives little indication—right from the first, with its fratricide and relentless head bashing—that the Creator's verdict is accurate. From the majestic cadences of Genesis 1, "Let there be," "and God saw that it was good," everything tends to go downhill once we go to work. The Creator has something other in mind, in calling all life into being and calling it "good" than what the Creator gets. Disobedience, rebellion, and blood are what the creature has in mind, "from youth" (Gen 8:21). And though the Creator gets angry, wreaks wrath, and storms off in a huff from time to time, for some reason the Creator keeps coming back to the creature, keeps resuming the conversation, keeps working with the creature who is, despite periodic bouts of good intention, hostile toward the very same God who gives life.

Because the story continues beyond our first rebellion in Genesis, we see that salvation is what God does from the beginning: "all things have been created through him and for him" (Col 1:16). Salvation is not some tactic that God had to devise after the disaster of our first rebellion in the Garden, God's Plan

B after we failed to follow Plan A in Eden. From the beginning, we are created for oneness with God and what God does with us, from the beginning, is atonement, "at-one-ment."

When we say "eternal life," that's a synonym for "God." God doesn't have an existence; God simply *is*. God is pure existence, complete life. When we say "death," that's a synonym for nothing happening and is thus an antonym for God. So when we say "God," we mean life, eternal life, that state of being where something's always and forever happening because God is life.

Only God has eternal life. Nothing in us or in the world is eternal. Among us, all that lives dies. End of story. Therefore, if we are to have eternal life, then we must somehow hitch on to God's life. To participate in God's life is to have eternal life, to be welcomed by God into God's existence, to be subsumed into God's story. And only God can do that. And whenever God does that, then that is eternal life. Here. Now.

The brief dialogue with Jesus and the criminal on the cross holds out the promise that, even in the worst situations of this life, it is possible to be with Jesus, here, now. What situation in our lives could be worse than hanging on a cross? Our God is not the sort of God who sits on high, aloof from the struggle and pain of this life. Our God gets mixed up in the mess of this life here on earth, even to the point of going with us criminals to the cross. If we want to be with God, in paradise or anywhere else, then we can expect to be with him at the cross. With this God, it gets very, very dark, and then we open our eyes and see that God is there, beside us. With this God, things go from bad to worse, from worse to awful, and then there, next to us, is God hanging in there with us, on a cross.

We need not sit around trying to envision some fuzzy, ethereal future in which we will "be with Jesus." That can all begin now, graciously made available to us, here, now. "*Today* you will be with me in Paradise" is not some promise for a possibility in the distant future, but it is a promise of what Christ can be for us here and now. We shouldn't therefore speak of the "afterlife" but of "eternal life," that life which is life with the living God, here, now. Even in the last moments of his life, that moment when he saw Jesus for who he was, the thief experienced paradise. He shined, even in this dark hour, the dying thief, suffering the same agony as Jesus, shined, his light made brighter in the reflection of Christ's eternal light.

So can you. Pay attention to those dark moments when you are forced by your discipleship to hang on some cross, when you are going through times of humiliation and pain because you are hanging out with Jesus. There, then, Jesus says to you as he said to the thief, "today you will be with me in Paradise." Paradise not one day, some day. Paradise now.

There is much that we do not know about Jesus Christ. The Gospels record only a few events of his ministry, and nearly all take place in no more than three years of his earthly life. Though obviously talking about the same Jesus, the Gospels differ on some details about him. The facts are few. Yet there is one thing we know for sure about Jesus, that on which all the Gospels agree: Jesus saves. It is as if the Gospels pare away everything from the words and deeds of Jesus that is not directly related to his saving work among us. Jesus saves.

His death is reported in all the Gospels not simply as an instance of the long history of injustice perpetrated by Gentiles against Jews (which his cross surely was) but also as a decisively significant part of the story of God's salvation of the world. And his resurrection is even more than God's defeat of death; his rising from the dead and his return to those who disappointed and betrayed him are a sign of God's vindication of Jesus as the God-given answer to the problem between us and God. Jesus saves. Paul's letters (the earliest of the writing about Jesus in the New Testament) say surprisingly little about the content of Jesus' teaching, still less about the signs and wonders that he performed. Yet all of Paul's letters—in discussing specific problems in early Christian communities, in working out the implications of his ministry—tell the world that Jesus saves.

The Gospels present Jesus Christ as constantly in motion, always on the road. In what direction does he journey? He is always relentlessly moving toward us. Whereas many religious leaders of the day sought to make careful distinctions between the righteous and the unrighteous, the saved and the damned, Jesus got into all manner of trouble (mostly with religious leaders!) for practicing unbounded hospitality. Many of the pious rejected Jesus for his disarming lack of discrimination between the presumed good and the allegedly bad. "This man eats and drinks with sinners and receives them!" was an early and persistent charge against Jesus.

Jesus provoked controversy by inviting himself to the table of sinners and in turn welcoming them to his. In response to criticism that he failed to exercise proper distinctions between the saved and the damned, those within the fold and those without, Jesus told a series of stories (Luke 15). There was the one about the shepherd who, having lost one sheep, abandoned his ninety-nine sheep safe in the fold and searched until he found the one lost sheep. A woman misplaced a single coin and turned her home upside down until she found it. And when she did, she called to her neighbors, "Rejoice with me! I have found that which I lost!" Then there was a father whose younger son arrogantly demanded his share of the inheritance, ran away to a remote country where he squandered every cent and, when he finally dragged back home in rags, was greeted by the father with the words, "Rejoice with me! My son who was dead is alive again. Let's have a party!"

Jesus told these parables in response to those who grumbled that the boundaries of his Kingdom were too broad, his reach too expansive. So we note yet another truth about Jesus. Not only does Jesus save, but he also saves the wrong people, people nobody thought could be saved, people nobody wanted saved. Jesus was such a relentless, determined Savior that he not only saved insiders, the daughters and sons of Israel who expected to be saved, but also reached beyond the boundaries, saving those outcasts, sinners, and pagan reprobates that insiders didn't really want to be saved.

Be careful of that word *faith*. In hearing the Letter to the Ephesians say that we are saved "through faith," we modern, pragmatic people are likely to hear this as some sort of call to action, some new technique, a program for our self-betterment. No. Wesley joined the great Protestant tradition in asserting that we are brought to God not by our faith in God but by God's faith for us. God gives us faith. In connecting salvation with faith Wesley showed, right at the beginning, that salvation is something that God does in us, not something done by us. Faith is not what we think or feel; faith is what God gives us, a work that God does through us. Our faith is a sign that God has indeed brought us to sure conviction that Jesus saves us, even us.

CHAPTER SIX

FOLLOWING JESUS

I am still haunted by a long conversation I had with a man who was a member of one of my early congregations. He told me that one evening, returning from a night of poker with pals, he had a stunning vision of the presence of the risen Christ. Christ appeared to him undeniably, vividly.

Yet though this event shook him and stirred him deeply, in ten years he had never told anyone about it before he told me, his pastor. I pressed him on his silence. Was he embarrassed? Was he fearful that others would mock him or fail to believe that this had happened to him?

"No," he explained, "the reason why I told no one was I was too afraid that it was true. And if it's true that Jesus was really real, that he had come personally to me, what then? I'd have to change my whole life. I'd have to become some kind of radical or something. And I love my wife and family and was scared I'd have to change, to be somebody else, and destroy my family, if the vision was real."

That conversation reminded me that there are all sorts of reasons for disbelieving the resurrection of crucified Jesus, reasons that have nothing to do with our being modern, scientific, critical people.

On a Sunday not long ago, I preached on forgiveness. The text was Jesus' counsel to forgive seventy times seven times (Matt. 18:21-35). As people filed out after the service, a woman came up to me and asked, in a voice that seemed to me to contain more than a touch of aggression, "Do you mean to tell me that God expects me to forgive my abusive husband who made my life hell for ten years until I got the guts to leave him?"

I immediately moved into a defensive stance, mumbling something about, "Well, that's a tough issue all right. And I can't possibly say everything that ought to be said on such a big subject. But I do feel, or at least it sounds to me like Jesus is saying, with his talk of so much forgiveness, that . . . I mean, he does tell us to forgive our enemies and I can't think of a much greater enemy for you than your ex-husband."

"Good," she said, "just checking!" and she proceeded confidently out the door.

That woman reminded me of my high vocation. It is not my task to protect her from the rigorous demands of discipleship, by paternalistically saying to her, "Oh, that's right. You are an abused woman. I'm sure Jesus did not intend for you to bear moral obligation. Your abuse makes you a victim, not a moral agent."

She refused to be let off the hook so easily. She refused to let me relieve her of her baptismal vocation, rejecting my rather blasphemous temptation to imply that Jesus did not know what he was doing when he called her to be a disciple.

On the night a squad of soldiers arrested him, Jesus mocked them, undaunted, asking if they were armed to the teeth to arrest him, an unarmed rabbi, as if he were a common thief. Ironically, the soldiers were not the only ones with swords. Peter, the most impetuous of Jesus' disciples, the "rock" upon which Jesus promised to build his church, whipped out a sword and nicked off a bit of an ear—despite Jesus' clear commandment that his disciples not carry weapons. Jesus cursed Peter: "Those who take up the sword die by the sword." That night, Jesus once again refused to practice violence, even in self-defense.

"Those who take up the sword die by the sword" is one of the truest proverbs of Jesus. Both the victor and the vanquished must finally submit to the power of the sword. The sword we thought we were using to secure ourselves becomes our ultimate defeat.

As everybody knows, there is no way to get anything really important done without swords. That's why we have the largest military budget of any nation in the world—to achieve security and then preemptively to spread peace and freedom everywhere. What war has been waged except from the very best of motives? To call Jesus a "Prince of Peace" is an oxymoron. A political leader who doesn't make war when national security is threatened is no prince. And peace that is based on anything other than a balance of military power is inconceivable.

Thus, one of the most perennially confusing qualities of Jesus was his refusal of violence. "If someone slaps you on the right cheek, offer them your left cheek as well. Some Roman soldier commands, 'Jew, carry my backpack a mile,' take it one mile more. Pray for your enemies! Bless those who persecute you! Do not resist the evil one!" As if to underscore that his kingdom was "not from here," Jesus healed the daughter of a despised Roman centurion. Was this any way to establish a new kingdom?

It would have been amazing enough if Jesus had said, "I always turn the other cheek when someone wrongs me," or "I refuse to return violence when violence is done to me." After all, Jesus is the Son of God, and we expect him to be nice. Unfortunately, Jesus commanded his disciples—us, those who presumed to follow him—to behave nonviolently. How do we get back at our enemies? "Love your enemies!" What are we to do when we are persecuted for following Jesus? "Pray for those who persecute you." Thus, we have many instances in the New Testament of people violating and killing the followers of Jesus. But we have not one single instance of any of his followers defending themselves against violence, except for Peter's inept, rebuked attempt at sword play.

This consistent, right-to-the-end, to-the-point-of-death nonviolence of Jesus has been that which Jesus' followers have most attempted to modify. When it comes to violence in service of a good cause, we deeply wish Jesus had said otherwise. There are many rationales for the "just war," or for self-defense, capital punishment, abortion, national security, or military strength. None of them, you will note, is able to make reference to Jesus or to the words or deeds of any of his first followers. You can argue that violence is sometimes effective, or justified by the circumstances, or a possible means to some better end, or practiced by every nation on the face of the earth—but you can't drag Jesus into the argument with you. This has always been a source of annoyance and has provoked some fancy intellectual footwork on the part of those who desire to justify violence. Sorry, Jesus just won't cooperate.

***

"Good is the enemy of great. And that is one of the key reasons why we have so little that becomes great." Thus begins Jim Collins's management book, *Good to Great*. Collins tells how eleven great companies overcame the mediocrity of being merely good and dared creatively to launch out and be great.

Yet Collins could as well have said that the Christian faith, with its stress upon goodness, particularly humble goodness, is the archenemy of great. It is not only that Christians are called to be good rather than great, called to be saints rather than heroes, but also there is built into the faith a deep suspicion of those who would be great. When my friend Stanley Hauerwas was named "The Best Theologian in America" by *Time*, Hauerwas thanked them for the honor and then told them that, as Christians, we don't consider "best" to be one of our categories. Jesus leans decidedly toward the "wretched of the earth" and has some choice, severe words for the high and the mighty, the best and the brightest.

Paul urges us, in Philippians, to renounce "selfish ambition." Perhaps the stress ought to be upon the adjective. It's the "self-ish" ambition that's of the wrong sort. Yet in the same letter Paul continually exhorts the faithful to think about and to embody all that is good, to have within us the very "mind of Christ." That sounds ambitious, spiritually speaking, and even if I earnestly desire self-improvement, that little qualifier "self" so quickly transmogrifies into "selfish." Paradoxically, it is that "mind of Christ" who "emptied himself, taking the form of a servant," that mind who so severely judges our ambition, even our ambition to be good, and makes it look selfish.

Two old men sitting in their synagogue during the Sabbath service overhear the loud lament of another worshiper near them: "God, be merciful to me, a nobody! God, forgive me, a nobody! God, help me, though I'm a nobody!"

One of the men looks at the other and asks, "Who's this who thinks he's such a nobody?"

Even in our honest confession of our sin, there can be the whiff of pride.

Addressing those "who trusted in themselves that they were righteous and regarded others with contempt," Jesus told a story of two men who went to the Temple to pray (Luke 18:9-14). One, a sleazy, good-for-nothing tax collector, collaborator with the Romans, and swindler of his own people, prayed, "God, be merciful to me a sinner." He had nothing, claimed nothing, and sought everything. He wasn't acting humble, he was publicly humiliated.

The other man, an outstanding, righteous, sacrificial, Bible-obeying person, prayed, "God, I thank you that I am not like other people: thieves, rogues, adulterers, or even this tax collector. I fast twice a week; I give a tenth of all my income." He is not only a good man, but a really good man who does what Jesus urged and goes the second mile in his living and his giving. His virtues he regards as gifts ("God, I thank you that...") rather than his achievements.

Still, Jesus lands a zinger in saying, "I tell you, this man (the cheating scoundrel) went down to his home justified rather than the other; for all who exalt themselves will be humbled, but all who humble themselves will be exalted."

What on earth are we supposed to do with that? "OK, gang, let's get out there and really be humble this week. Let's see if we can out-humble the Baptists." The tax collector's humility wasn't a virtue, something he had worked at. It was simply a realistic assessment of his situation. He was a failure at being righteous. He had no hope of setting things right between himself and God, except God.

One reason that Christians tend to move toward those on the boundaries, tend to feel responsibility for the hungry and the dispossessed is because we worship the sort of God who has moved toward us while we were famished and out on the boundaries. God looks upon us all, even us fortunate ones, as the hungry and dispossessed who need saving. This is just the sort of God who commands, "when you give a banquet, invite the poor, the crippled, the lame, and the blind. And you will be blessed" (Luke 14:13-14). Here is a God who, for some reason known only to the Trinity, loves to work the margins inhabited by the poor, the orphaned, and the widowed; the alien and sojourner; the dead and the good as dead in the ditch. It is of the nature of this God not only to invite the poor and dispossessed but also to be poor and dispossessed, to come to the margins, thus making the marginalized the center of his realm. "Truly I tell you, just as you did it unto the least of these . . . you did it unto me" (Matt 25:40).

The story "I once was lost but now am found" is the narrative that gives us a peculiar account of lost and found, a special responsibility to seek and to save the lost. If we want to be close to Jesus—and that's a good definition of a Christian, someone who wants to go where Jesus is—then we've got to go where he goes. Christians go to church in order never to forget that we were strangers and aliens out on the margins (Eph 2:19).

"You know the heart of an alien, for you were aliens in the land of Egypt" (Exod 23:9). We were lost and then found. That continuing memory of the dynamic of our salvation—lost then found—gives us a special relationship to the lost, the poor, and anybody who does not know the story of a God who, at great cost, reaches far out in order to bring to close embrace.

On the cross, Jesus gets into it with his mother. "Woman, behold thy son," he says to her. Mary, look at the child you are losing, the son that you are giving over for the sins of the world. Maternal love is that love that loves in order to give away. In Mary's case, it was particularly so. When Jesus was born, old Simeon had predicted, "A sword will also pierce your heart." From the first, it was not easy to be the mother of the Son of God. And now, even from the cross, Jesus is busy ripping apart families and breaking the hearts of mothers. Because he was obedient to the will of God, because Jesus did not waver from his God-ordained mission, he is a great pain to his family. "Woman, behold thy son."

In that day, in that part of the world, there were no social attachments as rigid or determinative as that of the family. Family origin determined your whole life, your complete identity, your entire future. So one of the most countercultural, revolutionary acts of Jesus was his sustained attack upon the family.

In a culture like our own, dominated by "family values," where we have nothing better to command our allegiance to than our own blood relatives, this is one of the good things the church does for many of us. In baptism, we are rescued from our family. Our families, as good as they are, are too narrow, too restricted. So in baptism we are adopted into a family large enough to make our lives more interesting.

"A new commandment I give to you that you love one another as I have loved you," he said elsewhere (John 13:34). Watch closely. Jesus is forming the first church, commanding us to live as if these foreigners were our relatives. Church is where we are thrown together with a bunch of strangers and are forced to call these people with whom we have no natural affinity, nothing in common, "brother," "sister."

So after this moment, never again could the world say *family* without Jesus' people thinking *church*.

On campus one evening, debating the future of our fraternities and sororities, this student says, "One reason why I love my fraternity is that it has forced me to be with a group of guys, many of whom I don't like—guys of a different race and culture from my own—and call these losers 'brother.' That's made me a better person than if I had been forced to stay with my own kind."

"I've never thought of a frat as a church," I said.

That day when they came to Jesus saying, "Your mother and your brothers are looking for you," Jesus responded saying, "Whoever does the will of my Father, he is my brother." In other words, Jesus is naming and claiming a new family for himself, that family made up of disciples. Now anybody who attempts to follow Jesus is one of the Family.

Mark said that while Jesus was hurrying down the road, a man stopped him and asked a deep theological question: "What must I do to inherit eternal life?" (Mark 10:17-31). One Gospel stated that the man was a "ruler"; another noted that he was "young." All agreed that he was "rich." At first Jesus brushed him off with, "You know what Scripture says—obey the Ten Commandments."

"I've obeyed all the commandments since I was a kid," replied the man. (Never broken a commandment? Who among us could say that? This man was not only successful in accumulating wealth; he was successful at morality too.)

Then Mark stated, "Jesus looked at him and loved him"— the only time that Jesus is said to have loved a specific individual. Then, in one of the wildest demands Jesus ever made of anybody (because "he loved him"?), Jesus told the man to "go, sell all you have, give it to the poor, then come, follow me."

With that, Mark said, the young man got depressed and departed, leaving Jesus to lament, "It is very difficult to save those who have lots of stuff."

While the North American in me is distinctly uneasy about Jesus treating affluent people in this brusque way, the Wesleyan in me loves Jesus' response to the man's big theological question. Refusing to be drawn into an intellectual bull session, some ethereal blather about "eternal life" (which Jesus discussed only rarely), Jesus hit the man not with ideas about eternity but with ethics here on earth—the Ten Commandments, redistribution of wealth, moral transformation, discipleship. Here this rather smug, successful person attempted to lure Jesus into abstract, speculative theology; and Jesus, after citing scripture, forced the man to talk about obedience and action. Jesus didn't urge him to "think," "ponder," or "reflect." Rather, he spoke to him only in active verbs: "Go...sell...give...follow me."

When Jesus rose from the dead the disciples were told, "Don't be afraid." Those who knew Jesus best, and were in turn known best by him, knew that, while friendship with Jesus is sweet, it is also demanding, difficult, and, at times, even fearsome.

As the Bible says, "It is a fearful thing to fall into the hands of the living God." Presumably, it's not fearful to fall into the hands of a dead god, an idol who never shocks or demands anything of you, who is no more than a fake, a godlet, a mere projection of your fondest desires and silliest wishes. Out in Galilee—a dusty, drab, out-of-the-way sort of place, just like where most of us live—the disciples of Jesus were encountered by the living God. That Jesus could not only give death the slip but also be in Galilee suggests that the risen Christ could show up anywhere, anytime. And that's scary.

Here is God, not as a high-sounding principle, a noble ideal, or a set of rock-solid beliefs. Here is God on the move, moving toward us; God defined by God, God ordering us to be on the move into the world with God. And that's a joyful thing—but more than a little scary too. When it dawns on you that the living God is none other than Jesus of Nazareth, the Messiah we didn't expect, the Savior we didn't want, God in motion—well, fear is a reasonable reaction.

The modern world has many ways of turning us in on ourselves, eventually to worship the dear little god within. Christianity, the religion evoked by Jesus, is a decidedly fierce means of wrenching us outward. We are not left alone peacefully to console ourselves with our sweet bromides, or to snuggle with allegedly beautiful Mother Nature, or even to close our eyes and hug humanity in general. A God whom we couldn't have thought up on our own has turned to us, reached to us, is revealed to be someone quite other than the God we would have if God were merely a figment of our imagination—God is a Jew from Nazareth who lived briefly, died violently, and rose unexpectedly. This God scared us to death but also thrilled us to life.

Family was always a problem for Jesus. "Family Values" was not his thing. As a baby, his paternity was in question, and his birth was an embarrassment for many. As a child, he had problems with parental authority. "You didn't know that I would be about my Daddy's business?" he impudently asked Joseph and Mary when they reprimanded him for making them mad with worry by hanging out at the temple and arguing theology (Luke 2:49). Poor Joe worried about his paternity. "Son, why have you treated us so?" his mother asked after their frantic search for Jesus. What did Mary and Joseph do to deserve a smart-mouthed teenager like Jesus?

And when he grew up, he and his mother were at a wedding party. When the wine gave out and Mary frantically entreated Jesus for help, he brushed her off with a "Woman, what does that have to do with you or me?" (John 2:4 AP). Not the right tone of voice to take with dear old Mom.

And when his ministry got started, he thought nothing of reaching into a family fishing business, and with a terse, "Follow me," demanding that these fishermen abandon their aging father in the boat and join him wandering about with his buddies (Matt. 4:19).

"I've come to turn father against son, mother against daughter," he threatened (Matt. 10:35 AP). And he did.

"Daddy just died," said a man to him one day. "I'll sign up with you after the funeral."

"Let the dead bury the dead," said Jesus, in love. "Follow me!" (Matt. 8:22 AP). This had to be the reason Norman Rockwell never painted Jesus.

Jesus Christ—the seeking shepherd, the waiting father, the searching woman, the persistent presence until the end of the age—is the majestic, all-powerful, sweeping generalization. He is the "Yes!" of God pronounced upon the whole broken world. Yet there is also our frail, responsive, small, but essential "yes." God's grand decision for us precedes our decisions for God. We can say "yes" only because God has said "Yes!" to us in Christ.

We are the first installment of a debt that has been and is being paid. The battle is not between equals, but it is still a fierce fight. Our redemption is a fact, though a not yet fully accomplished, utterly finished fact. This is a hopeful word to the world. The pain and injustice that we experience are not illusory, not fake. They are reminders that we are not there, have not arrived at the completeness of what God has in store for us, not yet. The divine verdict upon our sin has been reached—all are prisoners, all receive mercy—yet not all know that divine decree, not all live in the light of that decision. For those of us who know, those who don't know are our great burden and delight, our assignment, and our gift.

We are therefore not to take smug consolation in our knowledge of salvation. Rather, we are commissioned to "go," and to "tell" (Matthew 28:19-20). Evangelism is driven by the engine of God's salvation that demands to be announced to all. We neither rest nor retreat until every corner of God's creation gets the news of God's salvation. One reason why the church flags in its evangelistic drive is its mediocre soteriology. When God's great "Yes" degenerates into a constrained "perhaps," there is little urgency to tell the world. What we have to say to the world is deflated into a message about just another technique alongside all the others that that the world is busy pursuing already. This is not news. What's news is that in Jesus Christ God was reconciling the world to himself.

CHAPTER SEVEN

THE CHURCH AND THE WORLD

Early in my ministry I arrived at a hospital room where a woman in my church had just given birth. I had been told that "there were problems with the birth." A couple sat in the hospital room waiting for the doctor. The doctor appeared shortly after I arrived, and said to the new parents, "You have a new baby boy. But there are some problems. Your child has been born with Down Syndrome. Your baby also has a rather minor and correctable respiratory condition. My recommendation is for you to consider just letting nature take its course, and then in a few days there shouldn't be a problem."

The couple seemed confused by what the doctor told them.

"If the condition can be corrected, then we want it corrected," said the husband. His wife immediately nodded in agreement.

"You must understand that studies show that parents who keep these children have a high incidence of marital distress and separation. Is it fair for you to bring this sort of suffering upon your other two children?" said the doctor.

At the mention of the word "suffering" it was as if the doctor finally began speaking the woman's language. She said, "Our children have had every advantage in the world. They have really never known suffering, never had the opportunity to know it. I don't know if God's hand is in this or not, but I could certainly see why it would make sense for a child like this to be born into a family like ours. Our children will do just fine. When you think about it, this is really a great opportunity."

The doctor looked confused. He abruptly departed, with me following him out into the hall. "Reverend, I hope that you can talk some reason into them," said the doctor.

The couple was already using reason, but it was reasoning that was foreign to that of the doctor. For me, it was a vivid depiction of the way in which the church, at its best, is in the business of teaching a different language from that of the world. The church, through its stories, worship, and life together, teaches a different language whereby words like "suffering," words that are unredeemably negative in our society, change their substance. Here was a couple that had listened to a peculiar story, namely the life and death of Jesus Christ, in which suffering could be reasonably redemptive.

A bigshot businessman in our town was indicted for looting his company of millions, bringing thousands of his employees to ruin. To prepare for his federal court appearance, he got "saved" and proclaimed to the world, through his publicity agent, that he had "found Jesus."

(Am I being too cynical here?)

Well, who should I see on TV a month later, hosting a "Christian talk show," than this weeping, allegedly penitent thief! There he was, before God and everybody, Bible in hand, pious and sweet as a lamb.

It was more than I could take. "The creep!" I exclaimed to my wife, Patsy. "Is there no limit to his hypocrisy? Can you believe this?"

She, passing through the den, mumbled to me, "It's unbeliev-able the sort of creeps Jesus is willing to forgive. Even more incredible is the sort of creeps Jesus commands us to be church with."

She spoke the truth. If you think the family that you were born into is a pain, consider the family that we've been adopted into because of Jesus! I've said it before, I'll say it again: one of the toughest challenges of Jesus isn't just Jesus, it's Jesus' closest friends. Never forget that a major justification for the crucifixion of Jesus was the creepy company he kept.

Flannery O'Connor lived for a time alone and unknown in New York. She said that going to church in such an impersonal setting had its advantages. Upon returning from Mass at the Church of the Ascension on West 107th Street, she said of her time in church: "Although you see several people you wish you knew, you see thousands you're glad you don't know."

The other day at our church, a missionary took up a collection for the children of Haiti. We passed the plate, and the offering was counted. It wasn't enough, said the missionary. "I'm going to pass this plate one more time," she threatened, "and when I do, I want you to pray one more time that Jesus will help you to rec-ognize the faces of your own children."

Look around you just now, at these losers who gather at the foot of the cross, people whom you hardly know, much less have much in common with. Pray to God for the grace to be able to see these strangers as your siblings. Pray to God that they'll be given the grace to see you as a close relative. All of the inade-quacies and problems that you had growing up in your family are being healed. He who had no conventional family, he who sired no children, is busy forming the largest family the world has ever known.

Welcome home.

The gospels depict Jesus as assembling a new community, reconstituting a scattered Israel, recalling those who had been excluded, and inviting everyone to the table. Christian ethics is inherently ecclesial, communal. Israel knew there could be no Messiah without the constitution of a messianic community. God's peculiar means of saving the world is through a family, a people reconstituted by Jesus. This manner of salvation is fundamentally Jewish. The way that the world is to be reclaimed is through the formation of a holy people, a kingdom of priests that shall be a light to all nations. This prophetic language of election is enlisted by Christian communicators in places like 1 Peter 2 and applied to the church. In Scripture, God's way of being universal, for all people, is through a particular people, Israel and the church.

If Mark is the Gospel of the cross, then Matthew and Luke come to mind as Gospels of the new community in Christ. Great authority is given to the community in matters of ethics, but that authority rests upon the astounding promise that, "where two or three are gathered in my name, I am there among them" (Matt. 18:20). Great demands are placed upon the community because Jesus is with us until the very end of the age (Matt. 28:20). Church is the way Christians do politics, the way we present a living, breathing, political alternative to the powers that be.

Christians have no way of knowing what is "good" before we know the church. We are forbidden to hold some *a priori* notion of "justice," or "peace," or "righteousness," then to ask how the church might be helpful in enabling us to attain that notion. Rather, it is the church's witness to Jesus that gives content to such highsounding words. It teaches us to define words like "justice" as "thy kingdom come," "righteousness" not as "the greatest good for the greatest number" or "equal pay for equal work," but rather as "thy will be done on earth as it is in heaven." We do not desire to come to that modern place where we allegedly "think for ourselves"; rather we want to think with the saints, to think faithfully with the church, to submit all of our images of righteousness, success, and good to the scrutiny of the church's story of salvation in Jesus.

Wouldn't it have been more fitting for Jesus to have spoken his second word [to the thief on the cross] as a word of comfort or explanation to his disciples, those who loved him and had followed him to this end, rather than to this thief? After all, to have believed that Jesus is the Christ, the Anointed and Holy One of God, and now to see him whipped, bleeding in agony on a cross, it's a shock. Were our hopes in him ill-founded? Are the mocking soldiers and the screaming mob right in their scorn for this "savior" who now needs saving?

Of course, such a question is typical of us disciples. We keep having difficulty with Jesus' reach, particularly when its scope is beyond the bounds of the inner circle, the church, us. Let's be truthful now: few of us, his disciples, were close enough for him to address. We had made it very lonely up there, at the top of Calvary. Humiliated, naked, reviled by the world in the most public and degrading of tortures, Jesus had to talk to whomever was close at hand. His ministry, his sermons, and his actions had now cast him among the very worst of people, in the middle of two of the commonest of criminals. Family, friends, disciples were nowhere to be found when the going got rough and the beating began. Jesus was alone.

There was no one there to comfort him in his need. Peter, the "Rock" had disappeared. Nobody but this crook to counsel him, nobody to talk with but this terrorist.

"Lord, we will stand by you," said all of us at the table last night. But that was in the quiet comfort of the family. Out here, with a howling mob and the Romans at last taking action, we say nothing and Jesus hangs there alone—except for a thief.

Earlier, we had complained, "This man receives sinners and

eats with them." Now we might as well grumble, "The Savior receives sinners and dies with them."

Did he not say, "where two or three are gathered in my name, I am there"? I always thought that he meant that about prayer or worship. If just two or three of us gather at church on Sunday, he'll be there. I never knew that he meant it about dying thieves gathered on Calvary. Now, this day, in his Second Word, I see his point: *Where two or three good-for-nothing criminals are hanging out, like hanging on a cross, I am there.*

This, says the theologian Karl Barth, was the very first church. Church, like paradise, is wherever Jesus is with two or three of us. And look where he is now: on a cross. And look who is with him: criminals. Here, with two or three gathered with Jesus, is as church as church ever gets.

As Christians, we ought never to forget that we speak from a minority viewpoint—and always have. We are, in our speech, speaking against the presumed world of the majority. Therefore, in our assertions, we will not find many interpretive allies in the weapons of the world. The world is accustomed to getting its messages from psychology, the vaunted ego, or clear-eyed reason. Our message requires a miracle to make it comprehensible. Conflict and disruption are inherent in Christian discourse because the claimed stability of the world, the presumption by which the world carries on its business, is being challenged. We North American preachers today may be among the first generations in our context to realize that the political ground has shifted under our feet. We are no longer deferentially addressing a culture that can claim, even in its unguarded moments, to be "Christian." Every Sunday we are issuing a declaration of war against some of the most cherished idols of our culture. The world in which we live is adamantly set against the gospel—and always has been. This culture in which we work is arranged, in all sorts of subtle but powerful ways, against the claims that Jesus Christ is Lord—and always has been. The world is a world at war—and always has been. Sovereignty is under dispute—and always has been. Thus the Bible is full of violence and war, for there was something about Jesus that brought out the worst in the world. Christians are contentious. It is not because we want to be critical and contentious, but rather it is because of the inability of the presumptive world to relinquish its tight, imperialistic grip upon the imagination, that there is conflict. "Common sense," always a great foe of gospel foolishness, is really social consensus.

———

One night I had a graduate of the university speak to the undergraduates on how she had left a spectacularly successful job on Wall Street in order to return to seminary. She now worked in the mountains of West Virginia among a group of impoverished little congregations.

At the end of her talk, many of the undergraduates expressed anger at her. They told her she was "irresponsible," that she had "wasted a great education." In other words, they got the point. Such a pastor—such a fool—is a living reminder that the gospel is not establishment but revolt, not settled accommodation but rather destabilization of present arrangements.

As Bonhoeffer put it, it is no small thing that God "allowed himself to be pushed out of the world on a cross." Or again, Paul, "God chose what is foolish (*moria*) in the world to shame the wise" (1 Cor. 1:27).

One of the earliest of crucifixes shows Jesus on the cross with the head of an ass. The Letter to the Hebrews says that Christ was crucified "outside the city gate" (13:12). He was "outside" in more ways than one. He, who entered Jerusalem on an ass, died as an apparent failure.

There was a kind of playful foolishness in him and his teaching of wasted seeds in an act of thoughtless, random sowing. He told of an unproductive fig tree buried in a foot of manure, and for him it was a theological point.

He said that the kingdom of God is like the story of the man who gave a party where nobody came, so the lord of the banquet got mad and invited in all the folk whom you wouldn't be caught dead with on a Saturday night. That's the kingdom of God.

It wasn't that Jesus was being unreasonable, it was that he was exercising a different kind of rationality than that of the world. After one has made a statement like, "God was in Christ, reconciling the world to himself," then all worldly rationalities are thrown into conflict and everything is up for grabs.

Yet there is this relentless tendency for the Christian faith, in our hands, to be transformed from sign of outrage and contradiction, insubordination and usurpation, into (in Tom Wright's words) "the cement of social conformity." The temptation to be "conformed rather than transformed" (*contra* Rom. 12:2) is rather relentless. Church is forever in danger of degenerating into Rotary.

━━ण॥∫▥▸ ━ण॥∫▥▸ ━ण॥∫▥▸ ━ण॥∫▥▸ ━ण॥∫▥▸

"Take off that tie!" shouts an usher as I make my way in from the parking lot. "Do you take your latte with a touch of amaretto?" It is so much easier to change that which we fear (the gospel) than to risk change in ourselves by someone as challenging as Jesus.

Most rapidly growing congregations see themselves as aggressively innovative, making all things new. Churches that once prided themselves on being careful custodians of the past and cautious protectors of the status quo, have now become celebrators of and aggressive advocates for the current age. The eager discovery of "the next thing," once the province of theological liberals, has now become the specialty of so-called Evangelicals. Theological minimalism and reductionism among Evangelicals, where everything about the faith is reduced to "the message," conspire to produce a naive, enthusiastic embrace of the media of contemporary culture in worship with little worry that the content of Christian worship may be radically changed in the experiment.

Neophilia has become the status quo demanded by a capitalist economy. Neither Scripture nor the Christian tradition told these churches that "new" is the chief virtue of a church. What passes these days for new tends to be an uncritical capitulation to the culture, subservience to a "tradition" of the past three decades under the guise of innovation. In loving the new more than Jesus, we lay bare our deep accommodation to a capitalist culture. The market demands new in order to keep functioning. More consumers than believers, we shop for the "new and improved model" of faith "that works for me." Any church that acts like a shopping mall is sure to be treated that way.

We work within a culture of rugged individualists and fragmented communities. We are officially schooled in the notion that we are most fully ourselves when we are liberated, autonomous, on our own. We live under the modern myth that it is possible, even desirable, to live our lives without external, social determination. Ironically, that we think it desirable to live our lives without external, social determination is proof that our lives have been externally, socially determined by the culture of capitalist consumption. I did not on my own come up with the notion that I am a sovereign individual who has no greater purpose in life than to live exclusively for myself. Rather, this culture has formed me to believe that I have no other purpose in life other than the purpose I myself have chosen. The irony is that I did not choose the story that I have no purpose in life other than that which I have chosen.

The issue is not, Shall I be externally determined by some community of interpretation and authorization? The issue is, Which community will have its way with my life? Or perhaps more accurately, Will the community that determines, interprets, and authorizes me be worthy of my life?

Perhaps we ought to think of the church as schooling in desire, learning how to want the right things in the right way and the right proportions. Unfortunately, many simply think of the church as just another way to get our needs met. Church is where I get one-stop shopping for the satisfaction of all my spiritual longings and urges. A capitalist economy tends to commodify everything, even Jesus.

The church is not about "meeting my needs"; the church is also about judging my alleged "need," about giving me needs that I would not have had if I had not met Jesus.

We live in a society that has long since moved beyond the satisfaction of basic human needs to the gratification of all our wants and desires, and the expectation that it is my God-given right to have those wants satisfied. Those who put it politely, by saying that we have moved into a "consumer economy" or a "service economy," are simply noting that those activities and commodities that were once regarded as superfluous and unnecessary have now become the very basis of our economy. In other words, this is a bad neighborhood for those who hope to avoid the sin of greed.

What we don't need is central economic planning or new laws, more taxes or fewer good-paying jobs. What we need is something much more difficult to get than a Porsche—character. We need the sort of character that is able to look at the world and all it has to offer, and at certain key moments say simply, "Thank you, but I'm now satisfied." It takes a huge amount of moral stamina to be able to say, "Yes, we could afford it, but we are not going to buy it, because it does little to contribute to the basic goodness of our lives." We need to switch our economic thinking from the supply side to the desire side of the equation.

It's become downright morally heroic to be the sort of person who could say, "No, thanks. I've already got more than I can possibly consume responsibly." It's become a great parental achievement to say, "Yes, dear, we could afford it, but we love you so much we don't need to buy you that car," or "Trips to Vail to ski every Christmas are fine for Tommy's family but not fine for us. We live by a different story, expect different things of ourselves than Tommy's family."

As we have noted, we are consumers even when it comes to religion. Here, take this, pray that, attend this service, worship here, and you will feel better in the morning. This religious marketing may not be a totally bad thing. Consumers have certain desires and demands, certain expectations for quality, which could be potentially positive for a religious institution. Sometimes uncritical, undemanding congregations get the sermons they deserve!

Unfortunately, the consumer mentality is not a very attractive mental condition. The consumer almost never asks, when consuming, about the larger good. Consumption is mostly about fulfillment of personal desire. Furthermore, consumerism does not mesh well with the gospel. The Christian faith says that church is not about getting what we want but rather about getting what God wants. The Christian faith is God's idea of a good time.

CHAPTER EIGHT

WORSHIP

We would not have had such a problem with ourselves, would not have had to worry so much about a matter like pride, had we not been encountered by Jesus, the One who told us not only the truth about ourselves but also the truth about God. He told us that we were frail creatures who react to our immortality in inappropriate ways, who find ourselves gods of our own liking who promise to pump us up to appropriate size and durability. All of our strutting about, our preening and positioning, is only a kind of backhanded validation of the strong biblical truth that we are created as dust and to dust shall we return (Genesis 3:19).

The most moving moment in Sunday worship for me is when my people come forward, at Holy Communion, streaming down toward the altar, and there they hold out empty hands like little children, like the famished folk they really are, empty, needing a gift in the worst sort of way. I think that is one of the most difficult, countercultural gestures of Christian worship—outstretched empty hands. What's normal, and natural, is the clinched fist, the hands grabbing and holding tight to what they can get. What's strange, from the world's point of view, is the open-handed, needy, empty request for grace.

I submit to you that there is no way that people like us (we have our Master's degrees!) could hold out our empty, seeking hands had not the church taught us to do so, had not the church inculcated this honest gesture among us. This is who we are, says Jesus, not big, self-sufficient adults, but rather little children, naked, frail, empty, and hungry, needing a gracious God in the worst sort of way. You can't get into this Kingdom if you are all grown up and big and important. You can only come in through a very small door as an inept, bumbling, ignorant, and empty little child.

But most of all, Jesus tells us the truth about God. God is more than omnipotent, omniscient, and all those other nonbiblical attributes that we would like to ascribe to God. God is the lowest and the least, the little one, the wretched, the one who hangs in agony on a cross, the one who stoops down and washes our feet, the one who emptied himself in order to get down on our level, the one who rose and thereby shall raise us up as well.

If we would worship this God, if we would follow him down his narrow, Nazarene way rather than parade down the world's wide boulevards, there will be some stooping on our part, too.

Once upon a time I went out to a small rural church to baptize a twelve-year-old boy whom a pastor had been instructing in the faith. I was happy to oblige until the pastor said, "Jeremy very much wants to be immersed. Can you do that?"

"Er, uh, sure. I can do that," I said, unwilling to admit that I had rarely baptized anyone by immersion.

I arrived at the church that Sunday morning, and sure enough, there was the pastor standing on the front steps of the little church with a small boy.

"Jeremy, this is the bishop," the pastor said proudly. "It's an honor for you to be baptized by the bishop."

Young Jeremy looked me over and said only, "They tell me you don't do many of these. I'd feel better if we had a run-through beforehand."

"That was just what I was going to suggest," I said.

We went into the church's fellowship hall where the pastor showed me their newly purchased font, dressed up by a carpenter in the congregation, surrounded by pots of flowers. Jeremy said, "After you say the words, then you take my hand and lead me up these steps, and do you want me to take off my socks?"

"Er, uh, you can leave them on if you want," I said.

Well, we had a wonderful service that Sunday. I preached on baptism, the choir sang a baptismal anthem then the whole congregation recessed into the fellowship hall and gathered around the font. I went through the baptismal ritual. Then I asked Jeremy if he had anything to say to the congregation before his baptism.

"Yes, I do. I just want to say to all of you that I'm here today because of you. When my parents got divorced, I thought my world was over. But you stood by me. You told me the stories about Jesus. And I just want to say to you today thanks for what you did for me. I intend to make you proud as I'm going to try to live my life the way Jesus wants."

Though I'm now weeping profusely (Jeremy asked, as I led him up the steps into the pool, "Are you going to be OK?"), I baptized Jeremy and the church sang a great "Hallelujah!"

Baptism is God's word in water that saves. Not that the church necessarily says that we are saved by this ritual, but rather baptism gathers up all the meanings of Christian salvation and demonstrates those in word and water. The dying-rising dynamic that is signified in baptism is at the heart of salvation in Christ. The church promises that this has happened to you, is happening, will happen to you in your salvation.

One day, Jesus' critics, seeking to entrap him, asked, "Ought we pay taxes to Caesar?" It was a trick. If Jesus says, "yes, pay taxes," it will make him a collaborator with the Roman occupiers. If he says, "no," he could risk the Romans' wrath.

Instead, Jesus asks, "Who has a coin?" (His pockets are empty.) A coin is produced. "Whose image is stamped on the coin?"

"Caesar's," is the reply.

Jesus answers, "Then give to Caesar what is Caesar's; but you take care to give to God what is God's."

End of discussion. Did someone protest, "But you didn't answer the question, Jesus; just what is God's and what is Caesar's?" No, because the answer is self-evident. Every Jew knew by heart the words, "the earth is the Lord's and everything in it." They also knew the Genesis claim that each of us is stamped "in the image of God." Not much is left for Caesar to rule after such sweeping claims for the proprietorship of God.

Thus, Jesus, good, contentious Jew that he was, takes a discussion about the propriety of paying taxes to Caesar and frames it as a debate about the First Commandment. We are not permitted to bow to other gods. Every day the orthodox Jew must jump out of bed and learn again to "monotheize," to place absolutely nothing in the way of the worship of the one, true, only living God. Every time Christians worship "in Jesus' name," examination of our possible idolatries is our main business. Why Jesus? Why must otherwise potentially good things like our nation or our money be called into question? Why must some of our most widely held and cherished values be considered as possible diversions from worship of God?

Jesus answers with his words and his life. When asked about the greatest of all the commandments, Jesus gave a very Jewish answer, "Hear, O Israel, the Lord your God is one; and you shall love the Lord your God with all your heart, and with all your soul, and with all your mind, and with all your strength." In other words, the Lord God is not only one, but the one and only. To this Jesus added a second from Leviticus 19:18: "You shall love your neighbor as yourself."

In order to get neighbor love right, we must get God right. Love of God in Jesus Christ is rationale for love of neighbor as child of God. We can't call God "Father," as Jesus taught us to pray, without calling our neighbor "sister," "brother." However, there is an admittedly exclusive implication to this otherwise inclusive stance toward the world. We see it in Jesus' repeated warnings about the danger of idolatry. We cannot love God with everything we've got if we are preoccupied with love of God's chief competitors. We will never love the neighbor if we deify the state, for the state is what teaches us to regard our neighbors across the border as potential threats, as enemies. We are able to love only one Lord at a time. To believe that Jesus is God, that this wandering Jew from Nazareth is Savior of the world, God reconciling the world to God, is also to disbelieve that anyone or anything else can be.

I recall a fierce debate that erupted at an ecumenical gathering of clergy when it was suggested that we end the gathering by celebrating Holy Communion. Some objected to this intercommunion saying, "My church has a very high theology of the Eucharist and therefore I am not allowed to partake with those who are members of churches where there is a low eucharistic theology. I have such a high view of the Eucharist that I cannot celebrate the meal with those who have another theology of the sacrament."

But based upon Paul's corporeal reading of the Lord's Supper, it would seem that a "high" view of the Eucharist is that view that stresses the unity of Christians about the table of Christ. A "low" eucharistic theology is that which uses the table to draw lines of division between Christians.

My sense is that pastors will need to expend more of their pastoral energies, in a rootless, mobile society, pondering the requirements for truly Christian *koinonia*. On Sunday, those elements of worship, those rituals that help unite us, are to be emphasized. Those that fragment and isolate believers from one another are to be avoided. Individual glasses of wine at Communion, individual bits of bread, individual worshipers in silent meditation, solos rather than congregational hymns, are all questionable acts of communal worship in the light of this *koinonia* principle. Indeed, private meditation is best on other days, in other services of worship. Sunday is a day to get together, and the pastor, as the leader of worship, bears primary responsibility for gathering the church.

Mother Teresa was asked, "What do you say when you pray?" She responded, "I don't say anything. I listen."

Jesus said, "When you pray, when you go head-to-head with God, let the very first thing you say be, 'Thy name is holy, thy kingdom come, thy will be done.'" In other words, prayer is the gutsy willingness to let God be God in your life.

Some misconceptions: Prayer is not so much what we say but a determined willingness to let God have God's say. Prayer is not so much an articulation of what I want but rather a risk of being exposed to what God wants. Prayer is the possibility that I might be changed in the conversation. Note that in the Lord's Prayer, Jesus does not begin with us and our need but rather with God and God's nature, with exposure to the demands of a living God—thy name be hallowed, thy will be done, thy kingdom come, on earth as in heaven.

I remember the advertising slogan from years ago, "Prayer changes things," followed by the slogan, "And sometimes what prayer changes is us."

One of the last conversations that Jesus had was in the Garden of Gethsemane-a no-holds-barred, white-knuckled, blood-sweat-and-tears argument-a conversation that ended with Jesus', "Nevertheless, not my will but thine be done."

What faith, what courage to say that, and to pray that and to mean it!

I pray, "Lord, take away this cup from me. Deliver me from this distress. Save me from this dilemma. Solve this problem. Salve this pain. Er, (long pause) amen."

I want God to know my will, my will be done on earth and right now. But that's not prayer like Jesus taught us.

I told my Freshman Seminar, "We're almost mid-semester. I think it would be good to get some feedback on this course. Don't be bashful, speak up, give me some mid-course evaluation. How is the course going? How am I doing as your teacher?"

Immediately one said, "Sometimes you seem kinda disorganized." Another, "You let the discussion go on too long." Yet another, "Have you ever taught this course before?"

And I said, "You're just freshmen! What do you know?"

A few weeks ago I had lunch with a man who has suffered terribly from a painful back problem for as long as I have known him. At lunch, he looked different. I commented on how he looked: "Joe, have you finally gotten the medical treatment you needed to take away some of your back pain? You look like you feel better."

He replied, "No, I have not gotten the medical treatment I needed. I'm still in pain, but a few weeks ago, while in prayer, I prayed to God the prayer that I always have prayed, 'Lord, I beg you, take away some of my pain so that I may live without the suffering I've endured.' And you know what God said to me? 'Now what gave you the notion that I was against your being in some pain? Read the New Testament! I put people in pain! Live with it and show people through your life that the life I gave you is good.'"

There was someone who had been taught to pray by Jesus.

━━◖◗━━ ━━◖◗━━ ━━◖◗━━ ━━◖◗━━ ━━◖◗━━

And so I stand on Sunday before the table of the Lord and look out upon the gathered congregation. My pastoral perch is a good vantage point from which to assess the scope of God's saving work. From what I can see on Sunday, Jesus has gathered about him an insufficiently culled harvest. A motley crew, they are young and old, dignified and ridiculous, knowledgeable of Scripture and ignorant, well-informed and clueless. See them drawn toward the throne. They are all being drawn in the great dragnet of God's grace, all being pulled through the narrow needle's eye, all drawn by the majestic, bloody magnet of love that is Jesus Christ. All.

We have tried carefully to teach them to receive the sacrament standing up, hands outstretched. We have told them that contemporary liturgical reform has overcome our former penitential obsession at the Lord's Supper. But they are Methodists. They love to kneel for the Body and the Blood. They throw themselves down at the altar, doing with their bodies what they have only felt in their hearts and more than they have reasoned in their brains. The church has failed them in so many ways but at least the church has taught them this: they are empty-handed beggars, starving for food that they cannot obtain on their own. They must stoop a bit to receive this blessing from the one who blessed the spiritually poor. In a consumptive economy, just to know that is great wisdom.

Watch them kneel and hold out their hands in grateful wonder. They thrust forth their hands toward the table in eagerness. They come reaching for the gifts of bread and wine, as if their embrace by the suffering beggar who was the Son of God were the most natural thing in the world, as if Jesus died for them alone. There are so many differently reaching hands, so multifarious an array of need brought to the altar. I know them well enough to know that they come with wildly divergent understandings and misunderstandings of Jesus. And still Jesus feeds them all, giving them a small foretaste on this Sunday of that banquet that he intends to lavish upon them for all eternity. All.

Sometimes we hear questions like this about what happens in our churches in worship:

"Frankly, I just don't get much out of the Sunday morning thing. A lot of the time, I like the music, particularly when it's contemporary. But there is a lot that goes on Sunday morning that doesn't do much for me. Am I supposed to feel something? I would think that being a Christian is more than sitting and listening. It is also doing. What is the good of the praying and the singing and the sitting and listening?"

What is the chief end of humanity? The proper answer from the Westminster Confession: The chief end of humanity is to glorify God and enjoy him forever.

The Christian faith is a matter of God's offer of love in Christ and our response to that love. We respond to God's love with our loving acts of service toward those in need in the church and in the world. And yet we respond to God's love not only by loving deeds of service to others, but also by simply doing the things we do for God because God is God and we are God's children. We are called not simply to obey God but also to glorify God. Above all, we are called to enjoy God. We are called to worship.

Love is not love if it is simply a matter of obeying rules, running errands, and performing duties. Some things we do just because we enjoy being in the presence of our loved one. So we sing songs, write poetry, dance, clap our hands, share food, or simply prop up our feet and do nothing but enjoy being with one another. In these purposeless moments of sheer enjoyment, we come very close to what love is all about.

If someone asked a Christian, "What's the purpose of your worship? Why do you gather on Sunday and sing songs, dress up, kneel, march in processions, clap your hands, shed tears, speak, eat, and listen?" we could only say, "Because we are in love." The most serious, most delightful business of Christians, when you get down to it, is "to glorify God and to enjoy him forever." In other words, to worship. Whether we are glorifying and enjoying God in church with our music, sermons, baptisms, and prayers or doing so outside of church in our social concern, witnessing, and charity, it is all for one purpose: to glorify God and to enjoy him forever.

I can't put it better than one of the most "pointless" and wonderful of the psalms, the very last one:

> Praise the LORD!
> Praise God in his sanctuary;
>   praise him in his mighty firmament!
> Praise him for his mighty deeds;
>   praise him according to his exceeding greatness!
>
> Praise him with trumpet sound;
>   praise him with lute and harp!
> Praise him with tambourine and dance;
>   praise him with strings and pipe!
> Praise him with clanging cymbals;
>   praise him with loud clashing cymbals!
> Let everything that breathes praise the LORD!
> Praise the LORD! (Psalm 150)

Here is the heart of Christians at worship: pure praise done in love for the sheer enjoyment of a Creator who first loved and is therefore beloved.

CHAPTER NINE

PREACHERS

December, Second Sunday of Advent, a prickly text from Malachi, jerks me by my clerical collar, shakes me up and down, and speaks:

> But who can endure the day of his coming, and who can stand when he appears?
>
> For he is like a refiner's fire and like fullers' soap; . . . and he will purify the descendants of Levi and refine them like gold and silver, until they present offerings to the LORD in righteousness. Then the offering of Judah and Jerusalem will be pleasing to the LORD as in the days of old and as in former years. (Mal. 3:2-3)

Don't worry, I assured my December congregation, the prophet is not talking about you. A wrath-filled God is coming to the temple, but not for you. God is after those who make their living at the temple, *the clergy*. "He will purify the descendants of Levi and refine them . . . until they present offerings to the LORD in righteousness" (3:3). We priests, contemporary "descendants of Levi," who live off religion, praying, prophesying, preaching, making offering to God in behalf of the people squirm when Malachi raves about the "priests, who despise my name. You say, 'How have we despised your name?' . . . By thinking that the LORD's table may be despised I have no pleasure in you, says the

135

LORD I will not accept an offering from your hands" (1:6-7, 10). God says to us clergy, in essence, "You wear me out" (1:13).

"The lips of a priest should guard knowledge, and people should seek instruction from his mouth, for he is the messenger of the LORD of hosts. But you have turned aside from the way; you have caused many to stumble by your instruction" (2:7-8), says Malachi. (Here, of course, the prophet is speaking of clergy who are also professors of theology in seminaries.)

After the prophet takes a swipe at priests who have committed adultery and fooled around with various members of the choir (2:14-16; you can look it up), then begins the Advent call from Malachi. "Who can endure the day of [the LORD's] coming? . . . He is like a refiner's fire, . . . like . . . soap . . . and he will purify the descendants of Levi." (3:2-3).

Malachi, and the words of a Yahweh worn out by clergy and their self-justification, summons us preachers to examine the curious connection between the practice of homiletics and clerical ethics. Malachi calls us back (or is it *forward?*) to clerical lives grasped by something greater than ourselves or even our condescending desire to protect our people, namely our vocation to speak and to enact the Word of God among God's people. We would be better people, you and I, if we were more faithful preachers.

Homiletical habits—disciplined, weekly study; honesty and humility about what the text says and does not say; confidence in the ability of God to make our puny congregations worthy to hear God's Word; a weekly willingness to allow the Word to devastate the preacher before it lays a hand on the congregation—are habits, skills of the homiletical craft that form us preachers into better people than we would be if we had been left to our own devices. This is the sort of thing Paul was getting at when he told the Corinthians that it would have been nice if he could have preached to them with flattering, eloquent words but, being a preacher he singlemindedly "decided to know nothing among you except Jesus Christ, and him crucified" (1 Cor. 2:2).

We live in a culture of deceit. In such a time, it is easy to lose our way. Therefore we preachers would do well to cling to our vocation, to determine to know nothing save that which the church has called us to preach, to serve the Word before we bow before other gods.

Who could blame the great God for being worn out with us clergy (Mal. 1:13)? Our poor preaching, Malachi indicates, is not just a matter of lousy homiletical technique, it is also a failure of character, a moral matter of tragic proportions. Yet this scathing prophetic rebuke by Malachi of false prophesy is also combined with hopeful prophetic promise. The Lord may even yet purify us descendants of Levi, may soap us down, fire us up, call us back to our chief task—to be yoked so securely and joyously to the Word that in the process of proclamation of the Word, we become the Word as it dwells in us richly.

<hr />

The modern, essentially atheistic mentality despises mystery and considers enchantment and befuddlement an affront to its democratic right to know (and then to use) everything for purposes of individual fulfillment. The flattened mind loves lists, labels, solutions, sweeping propositions and practical principles. Vast, cosmic claims of the gospel are reduced to an answer to a question that, though it consumes contemporary North Americans, is hardly ever found in the Scripture: *what's in it for me?* The sovereign, free story of *God with us* is condensed to what can easily be managed, controlled, contained, and stabilized by me. Technopoly deludes us into thinking that there is a tool for everything, including preaching, if we can find it and buy into it.

Limiting our preaching to immediate, practical impact and instant, quantifiable results prohibits preaching from being uniquely biblical. PowerPoint Preaching pushes for a selection of timeless *general principles*—rather than relationship with a complex *person* who is on the move, moving through time, our time, yet not bound by our time, not bound even to our wise general principles.

As Bonhoeffer noted, preaching is where Jesus Christ takes up room, where he deems to make himself available to the church. In Christ, God's Word became a person before God's words became a book. Preaching doesn't merely describe Christ, or offer some accurate ideas about Christ, or suggest some principles derived from Christ but is Christ's self-appointed medium of presence.

The proclaimed word has its origin in the incarnation of Jesus Christ. It neither originates from truth once perceived nor from personal experience. It is not the reproduction of a specific set of feelings. The proclaimed word is the incarnate Christ himself, the thing itself. The preached Christ is both the Historical One and the Present One. The proclaimed word is not a medium of expression for something else, something that lies behind it, but rather is the Christ himself walking through his congregation as the word.

In preaching, we are moving people, little by little, Sunday by Sunday, toward new and otherwise unavailable descriptions of reality. We are on our way, in the sermon, toward a new heaven and a new earth, a new world. The pragmatic, typically American charge against Christian preaching is that Christians fail to "practice what you preach." To charge preaching with being hypocritical is not to understand the pushy, imperialistic quality of Christian preaching. Christian preaching is not merely the skillful description of the world as it is but a bold, visionary, and demanding call to be part of a world that is to be. The result of proclamation is performance and we are not, in most of our performances, there yet. Christian preachers are heralds who proclaim the true sovereignty of God in territory whose ownership is still under dispute. We are not there yet. Jesus Christ is Lord but not in fullness and completion. Therefore the easiest thing in the world is to point to the gap between what Christians profess ("Jesus Christ is Lord") and how we presently live ("The United States is Lord"). We are thus accused of hypocrisy in saying so much more than we are able to live. Of course we say more than we yet have.

Christians must not allow the charge of hypocrisy to bowdlerize our speech. We must not trim our proclamation to our meager abilities to embody it. In preaching, it's the listening, rather than the speaking, that can be the greatest risk. (Karl Barth even defines preaching as "speech which obediently listens" and describes the best of all churches as "the listening church.") It is the risk of having our little lives judged by bold, visionary, eschatological speech, the pain of having our world rocked by another world that comes sweeping in upon us in the sermon. To take up residence in a new world, to become a citizen of a new order, I must first hear about it. It's speaking that constructs a world, and it's hearing that changes the world. To charge us with the hypocrisy of not yet living what we profess is to demand that preaching be merely descriptive or interpretative rather than announcement.

No wonder PowerPoint Preaching is popular with us North Americans. It flatters my ego to be told, in effect, "Now here are some common sense principles that you, as a thinking, sensitive, empowered, self-sufficient modern person, will recognize as eternally useful." I then am invited by the preacher to pick and choose the principles that make sense to me. Rather than be coaxed into an alien story, or seduced into a new world, rather than hear a word that is not self-derived and not self-controlled, the preacher puts me in the driver's seat as the one who manages communication. This confirms my impression, engendered in me by a consumer culture, that religion is just another technique for getting what I want rather than a means of getting what God wants.

Preaching is thereby construed primarily as a product to be consumed. Through the adept presentation of information by rhetorical procedure, formulaic technique, and instrumental concern we get what the preacher judges to be "relevant" or "effective." Packaging is everything, and the best PowerPoint preacher is the one who cuts through all that irrelevant, archaic scriptural packaging and pointless, unprincipled biblical diversions, boiling everything down to *the message*: a set of abstract propositions and practical advice detached from the church that makes gospel propositions or advice work. The goal of preaching becomes motivation of the listener, who exclaims, "I got it!" The result is almost unavoidably a gospel that is privatized, trivialized, and reduced to a memo that everyone can "get" without moral transformation or inculcation into a community that has, as one of its major tasks, our indoctrination into the rigors of faithful Christian listening (that is, prayer). In orthodox Christian faith, the "message" is a Messenger. Therefore, most of us find that the gospel is more a matter of "it got me" than "I got it."

PowerPoint Preaching is often pushed as truly evangelistic preaching. As a preacher I am told that this method reassures anxious listeners— particularly the uninitiated listeners—providing them with a sense of intellectual certainty. "I got it," they murmur appreciatively on their way out of church. That is, they got a specific technique to take home and utilize in getting whatever they happen to want rather than Jesus. Thereby the embodied gospel is disembodied, abstracted from the story of the God who has, in Jesus Christ, "got" us. Preaching becomes subservient to the "real world" (that is, the governmentally sanctioned, officially defined world without God) of the omnivorous and always needy, modern consumer.

140

It's user-friendly Christianity as the triumph of the market. The congregation becomes another vendor of a "meaningful life" to individuals who come in, give a listen, take what techniques they can use, and then go home and have lunch with a minimum of fuss and bother. A primary way that the reigning order protects itself from the cosmic, imperialistic claims of the gospel is to marginalize religion, making it a purely personal matter of individual choice. We continue under the illusion that we are free to decide and to choose which principles we serve without ever noticing our enslavement to the one principle that holds us captive: in order to have a life in capitalism, we are fated to decide and to choose which life we shall have.

What to preach? The Saturday evening dilemma of the hapless modern preacher—what shall I say in a sermon?—may be a uniquely contemporary situation. Preachers, by the nature of their vocation, are those who speak because they have been told something to say. Can you imagine Paul pacing about his prison cell, agonizing because "I have nothing to say to First Church Corinth"?

Jesus warned his disciples that "they will arrest you and persecute you; they will hand you over to synagogues and prisons, and you will be brought before kings and governors because of my name." But then in the same breath he calls these persecutions "opportunity to testify" (Luke 21:13). Even the worst things that happen to a Christian are to be seen as opportunities to witness, a golden opportunity to preach. To prepare for such crucial speaking, Jesus commands avoidance of preparation. "So make up your minds not to prepare your defense in advance; for I will give you words and a wisdom that none of your opponents will be able to withstand or contradict" (Luke 21:14-15), I will give you words (literally in the Greek, "I will give you a mouth"). We have something to say because God speaks. "I believed, and so I spoke," says

Paul (2 Cor. 4:13). Or as Karl Barth puts it, "Cognizance becomes knowledge when man becomes a responsible witness." That is, we Christians think with our mouths open. We know, really know, that which we are able to speak, and we are able to speak only because God speaks.

If we will not be subservient to the Word, if we will not preach what the church has ordained us to preach, if we will not be tethered to the cross, we shall serve and be tethered to some god or other good. Let this narrative and the similar ones that have arisen in your experience be a reminder to us of the perils of poor preaching.

Luther was fond of contrasting a "theology of glory," in which the cross was seen as avoidable, optional equipment for Christians, with a "theology of the cross" which, according to Luther, calls things by their proper names and is unimpressed with most that impresses the world. To bear the cross of Christ is to bear its continual rebuke of the false gods to which we are tempted to give our lives. "Autosalvation" is the lie beneath most theologies of glory.

Yet to take up the cross of Christ, to be willing to assume a yoke of obedience upon our shoulders, oblivious to the praise or blame of our congregations, is also the basis of what it means to have life and that abundantly, to live one's life in the light of true glory come down from heaven in the person of Jesus the Christ.

Preachers must be flexible. The Bible is not God's Word in the sense of a state code that tells us precisely what the view of the state is. In reality we ought to say that the Bible *becomes* God's Word. Whenever it *becomes* God's Word, it is God's Word. What we have here is an event. Simply to have read somewhere that the Bible is God's Word is not the point. Preachers are summoned to a life history with the Bible in which something constantly takes place between them and God's Word. Flexibility means, then, that we have to plunge into this movement, submit to it, and let it lead us through the whole of scripture in all its statements and stages. The fact of the canon tells us simply that the church has regarded these scriptures as the place where we can expect to hear the voice of God. The proper attitude of preachers does not depend on whether or not they expect God to speak to them here.

Preaching is the proclamation of the Word of God. It is neither moral exhortation (the gospel is demeaned and our human situation is denied by reducing preaching to moral exhortation), nor a heartfelt expression of the preacher's personal piety (who cares?). Preaching is not a skillful representation of God's word (the task of theology). Preaching is not, despite the history of rhetoric, primarily a matter of persuasive speaking. Persuasive speaking is God's problem, not ours. A sower goes out to sow and, without careful preparation or planning, just begins slinging seed. Of course, in such effusive sowing, there is much waste, for this sower seems determined to overwhelm the world with words. In fact, most of the seed falls on infertile ground. It is up to God to give the growth, not us preachers. The hearing of God's word is not an example of democracy in action, with the hearers making savvy choices in what they will accept or reject. Preaching is dramatic, effusive presentation of God's word, so that God's word is heard through it, if God wills. Whether God speaks through preaching is God's free choice: Karl Barth says that "When and where it pleases God, it is God's own Word," but preaching is nevertheless that dangerous, confident adventure of letting God be God in the church.

143

Throughout the history of the church's preaching, one senses a certain nervousness within the church, a recurring lament about the current state of the church's preaching. The church is right to worry about its preaching because every Sunday sermon is a sort of experiment, a test, a public demonstration of the church's claim that Jesus Christ was indeed raised from the dead and continues to speak to the very ones who betrayed him. As Word of God, something that God says before we say anything, preaching is one of the three forms of God's revelation (preaching, scripture, and Christ—the Eternal Word) and a unique way that the Trinity communicates with us.

〜〜〜 〜〜〜 〜〜〜 〜〜〜 〜〜〜

As Isaiah says, "The grass withers, the flower fades," everything dissipates. We preachers can take heart in the reality that only one thing is eternal: "the word of our God will stand forever" (Isa 40:8). For the preacher, only one thing is eternal—the living word of a living God. To preach as a Christian is to claim *real presence*. Jesus was not a new idea. He was a new presence, a speaking, revealing presence. It was New Creation, not as mere renovation or extension of the old creation. The Galileans thought they heard a new teaching by Jesus (Mark 1:27) and the Athenians thought they heard, in Paul's address, something new (Acts 17:19). In a profound, yet inchoate way, they were right. A new One had come on the scene (Eph 2:15; Col 3:10), genuinely new. That "new [thing]" foretold by Isaiah (Isa 48:6), the "new heaven and new earth" of Revelation 21:1 was here, in God. Those who thought old wine is better than new (Luke 5:39) were wrong. There's a new commandment in town (John 13:34). "Behold I make all things new," says the one who now, after Resurrection, rules (Rev 21:5 KJV).

Humor is thus a part of Easter because, as is in so many good jokes, humor gives us a temporary escape from the bounds of history. In a joke, things don't end as they usually do in life. We are surprised. We smile. There is room, God-granted space between the determinations of history and time as God is making time God's. We are not to take the present too seriously, as if now is all there is that is going on in the world. Thus the saints once spoke of Easter as the great joke God played on the devil.

We are ultimately hopeful and humorous about the future because we already have seen the future. The One who is, and is yet to come, is also the one who has come. This new is not merely some future hope but is already present as event, as newly enacted here and now. That's what "kingdom of God is at hand" meant in the preaching of Jesus. In preaching, Jesus took time for us. In Easter, that which was concealed in the earthly life of Jesus was revealed, became present to us, now. That which was from before the foundation of the world (John 1) became real, now, whenever the Risen Christ slipped through locked doors and was present (John 20). We who were "once...far off " have "now...been brought near" (Eph 2:13). Whenever this story is preached, it is effected. Whenever anybody hears anything in a sermon, the kingdom of God has come near, now, death's grip on the world is broken—it's Easter all over again.

Surely that's why, though John could have written in his Gospel enough words about Jesus to fill more books than the world could contain, John wrote just these words that we might come to believe that Jesus is Messiah, Son of God, that we might have life here, now in his name (John 20:31). Jesus preached, "the time is fulfilled, and the kingdom of God has come near" (Mark 1:15) and Galatians 4:4 depicts Christ's birth as when "the time had fully come." "Behold, now is the acceptable time; behold, now is the day of salvation" (2 Cor 6:2 KJV).

Ancient words, spoken then, spoken to them, remembered, recollected from the past so that Christ might be present to us—it's a move that happens all the time in preaching.

When Paul preached at Antioch, people pled, "Please preach that sermon again next week" (Acts 13:42). What a curious request. Nobody ever said to me, "Great sermon! Let's do it one more time on Monday, same time, same place, same sermon."

It's even more curious when one considers Paul's sermon in Acts 13—an uncreative rehash of Paul's previous Acts sermons. Moreover, who was the audience for this sermon? Surely it was the church. In other words, the audience already knew the content of the sermon, had already heard it all before.

And yet, they asked Paul to say it again. Perhaps the church knew, even in its infancy, that faithful preaching is always repetitious reiteration, always preaching again.

A sermon is more like a workday breakfast than a fancy state dinner. Preaching ought to stick with us for the long term. A sermon is cumulative nourishment. Most of us shun innovation at breakfast. Nobody says, "Cornflakes with milk? *Again?*" Breakfast is not intended to be original or life changing. (Show me somebody who expects excitement at breakfast and I'll show you someone who...well...) Preaching is meant to be nourishment for the long haul, life sustaining. The story that preaching tells is renewing, but not new. Jesus said he was the "bread of life," not the flaming cherries jubilee of life. Ordinary bread sustains. One of the few things that Jesus gave us permission to pray for on a daily basis, by rote, repetitiously, without thinking about it, was bread.

I do wonder if we preachers engage in homiletical calisthenics in our sermons, devising all sorts of intellectual props for the gospel, because we are attempting to enable the gospel to make sense apart from the living, breathing, embodied Christian community that makes Scripture make sense. In other words, are we guilty of deluding ourselves into thinking that we must work hard to keep our preaching fresh and interesting when the main thing Scripture wants to do is to be edifying to the saints who are busy being scriptural people? Perhaps our greatest need in our biblical interpretation is not a better sense of eschatology but a more active engagement in mission? The goal of preaching is embodiment, discipleship more than mere intellectual assent or aesthetic appreciation.

I recently watched a violinist play Vivaldi. She was utterly absorbed by the music on the printed page, her whole body in motion from what she saw with her eyes, vision being transferred through the brain to her fingers, all conveyed to the instrument she played. While she was completely attentive, ardently faithful to each note on the page, she also gave the music an interpretation that was her own—she seemed to play the piece with particular energy and heightened tempo.

I thought this violinist was a good parable of us preachers. We preach while being thoroughly attentive to the biblical text, honoring the details, bowing to the specifics, playing the notes as they are printed, so to speak. But we also give the text our interpretation, both in what we say and how we say it. We want to be original, faithful to our own gifts and insights, but we want to be even more faithful to the text as we have received it. Our preaching is "repetition" in a manner similar to the way that violinist repeated Vivaldi.

What is God's kingdom like? A sower went forth to sow. Did he carefully plan, diligently preparing the soil for the seed? Hey, it's the kingdom of God! He slung seed everywhere, wasting lots of good seed with reckless abandon.

Of course, much of the seed is wasted—falling along the road (like I say, it was really messy agriculture), gobbled by birds, choked by weeds. Miraculously, some of the seed, a small minority, germinated, took root, and produced a rich harvest. Miraculous, considering all the seed had going against it. Though this seems to be poor agricultural productivity to me, Jesus found it thrilling.

As a preacher, working for Jesus the preacher, having nothing to arm me and help me fight my battles but words, desperately hoping for a hearing, this may be my favorite parable.

It takes great faith in Easter, particularly faith in the gift of the Holy Spirit, to be honest with our people that we have not a clue to the meaning of some biblical passage, or that we have no sense of a satisfying ending for a sermon, or that we are unsure of precisely what the congregation ought to do after hearing a given text. The most ethically dangerous time within a sermon is toward the end of the sermon, when we move from proclamation to application and act as if we know more than God. Sometimes we preachers are tempted to play God, to fill all the gaps between Jesus and our people, to make Christ too easily available to them, to dumb down discipleship. "Stewards of God's mysteries" (1 Cor. 4:1) ought not be too free in dispensing and disposing of the mystery that is Christ. We ought to preach in such a way that, if Jesus has not been raised from the dead, then our sermons are utterly incomprehensible. Faithful sermons require the presence of the Holy Spirit to make them work.

I am learning how to preach. I've only been trying to preach for the last thirty years and, after thirty years, I know less about how to preach a sermon than when I began.

I've learned that when it comes to sermons, people don't listen; more accurately, people don't hear—there are too many obstacles to successful communication. There's the skeptical modern world, science, attention deficit disorder, sophomore hormones, sin.

I work on a sermon, I do my homework. Then I stand up here and thrash about for twenty minutes. I tell some sappy stories. I gesture from the torso. But you don't hear! Even though the lights are in my eyes up here, I can see that you don't hear!

I don't know how to preach. I've tried every technique, different forms and arrangements. It's hard to hear the things of God, particularly things of God. How can you talk to someone about God? How do you speak in such a way that people don't just hear about God but are brought to God? I have learned that it is just about impossible to get people to get a sermon.

But sometimes, they do. People undeniably hear. Most of you keep coming back because, having had the lightning strike once, it could well strike again, and you want to be here for it. Having once shuffled in here—distracted, unfocused, unsure—you have, despite all, irrefutably heard.

You know what annoys me about all of you? It's when I preach a sermon, that I meant to be good, but it isn't, say a sermon that could have been a good sermon if I had only had a month more to work on it, a sermon like that—poorly illustrated, badly supported, turgid, and opaque—that sort of sermon, and here you come out, tears in your eyes, grip my hand, and say, "Thank you. That was wonderful. That was life-changing! Got it!"

Got what? I have the manuscript for that sermon. I'm an expert on preaching, and I know a bad sermon when I hear one. There's nothing there!

Now why, despite my worst efforts, did you hear? Who pulled back the veil between us and God? Not me.

A clergy friend of mine, for his sabbatical, didn't read books and write thoughts. He chose to travel about the country, visiting churches, listening to sermons. I asked him what he learned in his thirty-sermon tour, and he said, "I think it's a miracle that anybody ever hears anything."

And yet, you do. Why? I think it's a miracle.

When I was courting the Rev. Carl Parker's daughter (who eventually became my wife, Patsy), Mr. Parker was serving as a District Superintendent in the Marion District of the Methodist Church. I was nervous. I wanted to make a good impression. I was considering entering seminary in the fall, and I wanted the approval of this preacher's family.

Because a District Superintendent does not serve one congregation but supervises those preachers in the district, Mr. Parker spent many Sundays in the pew rather than in the pulpit, a situation that he detested. On one particular Sunday, the preacher was a master of ambiguity and equivocation. Mr. Parker squirmed in his pew as the preacher carefully qualified just about every statement made in the sermon. At five-minute intervals throughout the sermon, Mr. Parker withdrew his large railroad watch from his pocket, the watch that had been given to him by some thankful congregation of the past. He would gaze at his watch, remain surprised that so little time had passed, close it, shake his head, thrust it back into his pocket, and groan slightly.

The poor preacher continued to flail away, thrashing at his subject, rather than delivering it. "We need to be more committed to Christ...but not to the point of fanaticism, not to the point of neglect of our other important responsibilities. We need to have a greater dedication to the work of the church. Now I don't mean that the church is the only significant organization of which you are a member. Most of us have obligations to various community groups...." And on, and on.

After service, all of us in the District Superintendent's party brushed right past Mr. Milk Toast with barely a word of greeting. Mr. Parker led us down the sidewalk back to the district parsonage, like ducks in a row. He went right through the front door and charged up the stairs. Pausing midway, he whirled around, shaking a finger at me and thundering, "Young man, if God should be calling you into the pastoral ministry, and if you should ever be given a church by the bishop, and if God ever gives you a word to say, for God's sake would you say it!"

Mainline Protestantism seems to be suffering from a failure of theological nerve. Our trumpets suffer from our uncertain sound—the bland leading the bland. Courage to speak arises, in great part, from the conviction that God has given us something to say. I recall Leander Keck (in a debate on the most effective sermon styles) saying, "When the messenger is gripped by a Message, the messenger will find the means to speak it." As preachers, we know the challenge in a relativistic culture of standing up and saying, "This news is good, this word is true."

On one occasion Walter Brueggemann said, "If you are a coward by nature, don't worry. We can still use you. You can get down behind the biblical text. You can peek out from behind the text, saying, 'I don't know if I would say this, but I do think the text does.'" I like that image—the preacher hunkered down, taking cover behind the biblical text, speaking a word not of the preacher's devising.

Courage to speak requires clarity about our source of authority. If we only stand in the pulpit to "share" or to "tell my story," as some misguided recent homiletics have urged us, then the church shall end, not with a bang but in a simpering sigh after a thousand qualifications and reservations. This Sunday, take Mr. Parker's advice. If God gives you a word for God's people, for God's sake, say it!

CHAPTER TEN

PASTORS

Before the altar of God, at the bedside of the sick, in conversation with troubled souls, befuddled before the biblical text, there is the pastor. Standing in that fateful intersection between God's people and God, at that risky transaction between Christ and his Body, the church, stands the priest. It is no small thing to be in mediation between God and humanity, to offer the gifts of God's people, to intercede for the suffering of the world in prayer, rightly to divide the Word of God. With trembling and with joy, the pastor works that fateful space between here and the throne of God. This yoke, while not always as easy as Jesus implies, is often quite joyful. It is a joyful thing to be a pastor, to have one's life drawn toward dealings that are divine; to bear burdens that are, while not always light, at least more significant than those that the world tries to lay upon our backs. It is a joy to be expended in some vocation that is greater than one's self.

⸻ ⸻ ⸻ ⸻ ⸻

I know a pastor who called it quits by standing up without warning in a vestry meeting and announcing that he was leaving the priesthood. After the initial shock, an older member of the vestry asked, "Don't you think you owe us an explanation?"

He replied that he had entered the ministry to preach the gospel and to support the people of Christ in their discipleship. Yet over the years, his ministry had become little more than a boring matter of housekeeping and dull routine. He couldn't take it anymore, so he was leaving.

"Did it ever occur to you that many of us are bored too?" the church member persisted. "None of us have asked you to preach dull sermons. You do the things you do in ministry because that's what you do, not because we have demanded it. If you have some higher, more interesting and bold idea of what church ought to be, tell us. Some of us feel the same way you do about what this congregation's become."

With that began a discussion that continued well into the night concerning the point of the church, the purpose of ministry, and the message of the gospel. The priest stayed. The church was born again. Too many of us pastors too passively acquiesce into dull, theologically indefensible forms of ministry that trivialize our vocation, cause us to neglect our marriages and families, and ultimately lead to despair. One of the necessary pastoral tasks is forming congregations whose vision of the church gives dignity and validation to the sacrifices we make in being pastors.

<hr/>

Ministry is not a "profession," as the term is often used. While it is important for ministers to be competent and proficient in the tasks of ministry, the deep difficulty suffered by two corrupted professions today—law and medicine—warns us that a profession was first a moral matter. A profession is a matter of someone being formed into an exemplary person by being attached to a noble body of belief like jurisprudence or care of the sick. We have degraded "professionals" by making them primarily people who know something that the rest of us do not, rather than being people who the rest of us are not.

In one important sense clergy are members of a profession. The designation "professional" was first applied to clergy. A professional was first a person who had something to profess, some body of knowledge, an allegiance to some notion of the higher good, some attachment to goods and goals more significant than the self. One of the deep problems with the two "professions" of medicine and law today is that doctors and lawyers often appear to have nothing more significant to "profess" than their patients and clients. Medicine and law think that their primary purpose is to serve consumers, rather than public health or jurisprudence. Pastors profess God. Pastors are accountable to God; the test of their work is someone more significant even than their parishioners. In all their pastoral work, pastors are professing faith in God, not in the supposed needs of their people.

Ministry is not merely a profession, not only because one cannot pay pastors to do many of the things they routinely do, but also because ministry is a vocation. Ministers are more than those who are credentialed and validated by the approval of their fellow members of their profession. Ministers must be called. True, Christians believe that all occupations ought to answer to the vocational question, namely, How is this work an extension of your Christian discipleship? For clergy, this sense of vocational responsibility is crucial due to the peculiar demands upon ministers.

Pastors, like doctors and lawyers, deal with matters that really matter, like sex, marriage, death, and salvation. Because so much is at stake in these matters, and because the issues involved are rarely clear-cut, not only is wise discernment required, but also good judgment, an ability to know each situation on its own, and above all, honest self-knowledge. Aristotle . . . stressed that good works arise from good people. In order to do good, one must gain wisdom, experience, and self-control. He noted that some of the best things we do as people occur not because we have rationally thought through all possible alternatives, not because we have adhered to some moral code or set of principles, but simply because we responded out of habit, out of an ingrained, inculcated pattern of living. Our actions were "second nature" to us, congruent with who we are and who we hope to be. This, said Aristotle, is ethics worthy of the name.

In so many ways, ministry is difficult because it is about the construction, the evocation, the invocation of another world. In the most unassuming manner, Christian ministry provokes a collision with so many of the values held dear in this society. That which we are taught to name as the kingdom of God is at odds with our kingdoms. Although I in no way mean this as justification of low clergy salaries, that many ministers are highly trained and often poorly paid is itself an affront to a culture that believes that a person's worth is measured in money.

Seminarians are forever complaining about the gap between their expectations for the church, as engendered in seminary, and the reality of the church they experience as new pastors. That gap between the sociological reality of the church and the theological vocation of the church is necessary and even admirable. It is part of the pastor's vocation to keep working that space, to keep noting that gap between who the church is and who the church ought, by God's grace, to be—and will, by God, be someday.

⋘ ⋙ ⋘ ⋙ ⋘ ⋙ ⋘ ⋙ ⋘ ⋙

I am troubled when a seminarian tells me that she or he is going into the Christian ministry because, "I like helping people." "Helping people," may be a satisfactory basis for ministerial work, if ministry is practiced in a place like Honduras, the second poorest country in the Western Hemisphere. In such a context, people have interesting needs that deserve our help—needs like food, clothing, and housing.

But in an affluent, consumerist, capitalist culture, attempting to "help people" becomes extremely problematic among the relatively well off. Many of us, having solved so many basic human problems like food, clothing, and housing, now move on to less interesting infatuations. We live in a polity, ruled over by the Constitution, that tells us that we are born with certain inalienable "rights." The Constitution created a definition of a human being as a bundle of rights. The purpose of government is to give us the maximum amount of space to assert and to fulfill our rights. Government enables me to express my rights, without ever making a judgment upon the goodness of these rights.

A major difficulty with this arrangement is that, in this culture, desire becomes elevated to the level of need, and need becomes further elevated to the level of rights. And because we tend to be a pit of bottomless desire, there is no end to our need. Our list of rights seems constantly to expand, driven as it is, not by some public discussion about which rights are worth having, but rather by our relentless desire. Our culture tends to be a vast supermarket of desire. Anyone who goes out to meet my needs is going to be working full time!

I believe this is one reason many pastors are so fatigued. They are expending their lives, running about in such busyness, attempting to service the needs of essentially selfish, self-centered consumers, without critique or limit of those needs. Flannery O'Connor mocked a clergyman of her acquaintance whom she called "one part minister and three parts masseuse."

───◈─── ───◈─── ───◈─── ───◈─── ───◈───

Many have noted that we live in a therapeutic culture where all human problems are reduced to sickness. We want not so much to be saved or changed, but rather to feel better about ourselves. Harry Emerson Fosdick once called preaching "counseling on a group scale." The pastor becomes not the teacher or the preacher or the moral guide, but rather the therapist who helps evoke spiritually-inclined sentiments in individuals—soothing anxiety, caring for the distressed, and healing the maladjusted.

Certainly, the pastor is to care for people. But the pastor cares "in the name of Christ," which may give a different cast and set different goals for the pastor's care than for that of a secular therapist. What the Christian faith might define as "a well-functioning personality" might be considerably at odds with contemporary definitions of mental health.

I recall a contemporary historian, recounting in some detail Martin Luther King Jr.'s rather persistent attempts to win the praise of his father, "Daddy King." So much of the younger King's life can be explained, said the historian, as his tortured efforts to please a father who was very difficult please.

"Well, then, thank God Martin never got well adjusted," shouted an old preacher from the rear of the room. Thank God, indeed. A certain dissonance with the world, a holy kind of discontent, seems to be fertile ground for God's prophets. Truth is superior even to mental health.

Lacking theological control on our "care," we lapse into secular goals and techniques of care. We offer the church care that is not too different from that which might be received from any well-meaning secular therapist. The pastor is reduced to the level of the soother of anxieties brought on by the dilemmas of affluence, rather than the caller of persons to salvation.

There seems to be today a renewed stress upon spiritual disciplines, and the cultivation of those practices of prayer, meditation, and devotion that are gifts to all Christians, enabling us to persevere.

When I moved from parish ministry to campus ministry, I suddenly found a great need for some intentional, focused time, at the beginning of my workday, for devotion and reflection. For me this meant reading a group of collects from the *Book of Common Prayer* and praying a couple of the psalms before doing any other pastoral activity.

These acts of devotion helped to focus my work, served as a reminder to me of my peculiar identity as a priest in this academic setting, and gave me the authorization I needed to be on campus functioning not as a lower-level academic functionary, but as someone who looks for, points to, and talks about God. Such are the gifts of the spiritual disciplines.

Our extravagant claim is that through obedience to these crucial ("crucial" literally means *cross*) practices, Jesus gives us the resources we need to be faithful disciples. And we will never know whether or not Jesus was speaking truthfully if we pastors refuse to hold ourselves attached and accountable to Jesus' demands. Is the cross God's true way with the world or not? We shall never know unless we attempt to live lives based upon the cross.

Fortunately, as I enter into the struggles of my people, I have considerably more to offer than myself. I have the witness of the saints, the faith of the church, the wisdom of the ages. A pastor must therefore be prejudiced toward the faith of the church. One does not have to be a traditionalist to be a pastor, but it helps, particularly in a culture of "neophiles" (as Margaret Mead once called us), incurable lovers of the new who believe that old is bad and new is good. My frequent references to dead people is a way of witnessing that the church lives by the lives of the saints.

I am not free to rummage about in other texts before I have submitted to the biblical text. I am not at liberty to acknowledge as source of ultimate truth those contemporary, culturally sanctioned sources such as psychology, sociology, economics, and so forth before I have done service to the historic faith of the church. It is fair to have a lover's quarrel with the tradition of the church, to wrestle with and to question which tradition is sanctioned by God and which is spurious irrelevancy. Yet it is not fair to place oneself or one's culture above the story of Jesus of Nazareth as represented in the creeds, councils, and faith of the church.

Ironically, it is powerful freedom to know who claims your ultimate allegiance, to whom you are finally accountable. Our seminarians complain that, upon graduation from seminary, they are overwhelmed by the gap between the church that they expected and the church that they got. I am unimpressed that there is a huge gap between the theological definition of ministry and its sociological reality. As Richard Neuhaus says in the opening pages of *Freedom for Ministry*, his classic book on ministry, "there is a necessary awkwardness about Christian ministry because we are ambassadors of a 'disputed sovereignty.'" That "necessary awkwardness," that persistent sense that we are representatives of a sovereign who is in contention with the reigning principalities and powers, is a major source of all ethics worthy of the name Christian. The gospel is inherently countercultural and conflictual with all cultures, including the very first culture in which it made its way, and including the culture called the church that seeks to domesticate the gospel. Service to that gospel is bound to be countercultural because the gospel itself engenders a "culture" with its own distinctive symbols, language, myths, and ethic. The great challenge of the Christian ministry, since its inception, is how to work within a given culture without being subsumed by it. It takes great character to do so. The other great challenge is that, by nature, none of us is born well-suited to the ministry. *Diakonia* is against our natural inclination.

One of the burdens of the pastoral ministry today is that pastors, realizing that they have few skills or little esoteric knowledge not readily available to all Christians, attempt to be extraordinarily nice. The pastor is the Christian who is incredibly warm, affirming, understanding, patient, and popular. This is a curious reworking of the older image of the pastor as the vicarious saint of the congregation, the person who is paid to be more saintly than all the other saints. Pastors can be preserved from this perversion only by cultivating the awareness that ministry receives its significance from what needs to happen in the church, that its power proceeds, not from the pleasing personality of the pastor, but from the authorization of God through the church and table, who has the last say in the validation of your ministry. One of the great challenges of contemporary pastoral ministry is having something more important to do in our ministry than simply offering love and service to our people. Too many pastors never rise above simple congregational maintenance, never have any higher goal in their ministry than mushy, ill-defined "love" or "service." To find ourselves yoked, bound to our profession of faith, namely, that Christ really is present in Word and Sacrament, overturning the world through us; this is great grace.

Because the Christian ministry is significantly *countercultural*, at some odds with the predominate culture, including the very first cultures of Israel and Rome in which we found ourselves, we must guard against styles of Christian leadership that are essentially accommodationist. To be sure, we can never escape our culture. Yet all cultures stand under the judgment of God, including the "culture" called *the church*. Therefore, pastors ought always to expect some dissonance, a degree of abrasion with the culture—both social and congregational—in which they work. In attempting to be "relevant" to the world, we have sometimes been guilty of offering the world little that the world could not have had through purely secular leadership. First Peter 2:11 encourages us to live "as aliens and exiles." I believe that the contemporary North American church finds itself in a situation akin to exile, missionaries in the very culture that we thought we had created and made safe for Christianity. Therefore, I find much to be commended in the image of the pastor as a missionary, or more accurately, a lead missionary or equipper of the missionaries. We are no longer keeping house in an essentially hospitable and receptive culture, if we ever were. The African American church could tell the rest of us a thing or two about what it means to live as "strangers in a strange land." Today, even those of us pastors in mainline Protestantism are beginning to feel like the leaders of an outpost, an enclave of an alien culture within a majority, non-Christian culture. I therefore predict more of a pastor's time will be spent in the education, formation, and enculturation of the members of the congregation to be people who know how to analyze the corrosive acids within the surrounding and essentially indifferent—at times openly hostile—dominant culture. More of our efforts will need to be expended in giving our people the means to resist, to live by, and to creatively communicate the gospel in a world where Christians are a cognitive minority.

How can clergy possibly persevere amid the great demands of the church? Paradoxically, one of our major moral resources is the church—the church that has ordained us, called us forth to leadership, keeps calling us, keeps authorizing us, keeps empowering us to be better than we would have been if we had been left to our own devices. In expecting us to be truthful, courageous preachers, the church makes us truthful and courageous. In the church's weekly routine of worship, forcing us to worship a real God every seven days whether we feel like it or not, the church keeps some of us close to the wellsprings of the faith even when we have been negligent to avail ourselves of those restorative waters. In demanding that we stand between them and God, our people make us priests, and we are thereby surprised by our own priestly effectiveness, despite ourselves.

Being effective "despite ourselves" is one of the great gifts of being a pastor. Not long ago, when someone was busy taking me apart at the front door of the church after a sermon, I thought to myself, "That's rather amazing. I, who seem to be constitutionally conditioned to want to please everyone, have actually angered someone because I said what was maddening but true. This church has actually made good old, compromised, flatterer me into one who can sometimes be a speaker of truth."

The gospel is not simply about meeting people's needs. The gospel is also a critique of our needs, an attempt to give us needs worth having. The Bible appears to have little interest in so many of the needs and desires that consume present-day North Americans. Therefore, Christian pastoral care will be about much more than meeting people's needs. It will also be about indoctrination, inculturation, which is also—from the peculiar viewpoint of the gospel—care. Our care must form people into the sort of people who have had their needs rearranged in the light of Christ.

The call of Paul the apostle was his experience of finding himself living in a whole new world that had been inaugurated when Christ gave death the slip at Easter. Paul changed because of his realization that, in the resurrection of Jesus Christ, the world had changed, therefore he had to change or appear bafflingly out of step with reality (2 Cor. 5:17-18). That many ministers base their ministry on models of leadership uncritically borrowed from the latest fads in business leadership or therapeutic practices is yet another testimony to our failure to believe that God raised Jesus Christ from the dead, thus radically changing the world. In other words, our care cannot be detached from our politics. Our conviction about who is in charge cannot be disjoined from the call to conversion, the church's challenge to live in the light of Easter.

Sometimes one hears those in authority in the church tell pastors, "The most important thing is for you to love your people. Just be with your people in love, and everything else will work out."

Not necessarily. More difficult even than loving one's people can be the love of Christ, a truthful love that is the source of, and judgment upon, all our loves. We must be linked to something more significant than a vague notion of loving our people if ministry is to be service to the resurrected Christ rather than servility to the praise or blame of our people. After telling the church at Corinth to regard him and his fellow workers as "servants of Christ and stewards of the mysteries of God" (note he does not say "servants of the people and stewards of congregational finances"), Paul attacks the Corinthians, telling them, "But with me it is a very small thing that I should be judged by you or by any human court. I do not even judge myself. I am not aware of anything against myself, but I am not thereby acquitted. It is the Lord who judges me" (1 Cor. 4:3-4). We care for others under the judgments of Christ. Perhaps that is why pastors are also prophets. There is some sort of pastoral significance that the New Testament word for "compassion" (*splanchna*—Mark 1:41—from whence we get our word "spleen") is the same word for "guts." There is no way to be a truly compassionate pastor without being a truthful, gutsy prophet.

Throughout 1 Corinthians, Paul keeps calling the church at Corinth back to the authority of the gospel (11:16, 23; 15:3). Paul serves his congregation by being utterly submissive, not to them, but to the apostolic tradition. So should we.

Those who have kept at the Christian ministry longer than I will confirm the essential virtue of humor. One can be a pastor with only modest intellectual abilities, but one cannot remain a pastor for long without a sense of humor. The ability to laugh at life's incongruities, to take God seriously but not ourselves, to embrace the strangeness of our people instead of strangling them to death with our bare hands is great grace. Without humor, a bishop could be an insufferable bore, a district superintendent could be dangerous, and a pastor would be in a perpetual state of depression due to the state of the church. Humor is the grace to put our problems in perspective, to sit lightly upon our clerical status, to be reminded that Jesus really did need to save us, seeing as we have so little means to save ourselves. Humor is just a glimpse, on a human scale, of the way God looks upon us from God's unfathomable grace. As has often been said, the essence of sin is to take ourselves too seriously. Forgiveness and humor appear to be close kin, certainly humor is quite close to grace.

There is a close connection between the disruptive quality of humor and Jesus' primary means of communication, the parable. John Dominic Crossan demonstrated how Jesus' parables assault rather than establish a "world." A parable typically takes the predominant, officially sanctioned view of reality within a given culture, the "world," and then subverts that world. The surprise endings of many parables are close cousins to the endings of jokes. The gospel, in order to make its way in the world, must subvert the received world. Pastors, if they are half faithful, must be forever challenging the received world of their people. Effective pastors are often masters at irony, satire, and other forms of linguistic subversion.

Some pastors are, by their very existence, parables that challenge the world's story of what is going on in the world. "I love my pastor," said an enthusiastic undergraduate. "He is your typical, perfect pastor, always late for meetings, office always a wreck, books and papers all over the front seat of his car. He called me last night after midnight to see how I was getting along in college."

I wondered at the effect of this pastor—one so full of disorder and procrastination—upon this punctilious, precise, orderly undergraduate. Perhaps his raucous life hints to her of the possibility of a more gracious, less driven existence.

I suppose that humor is a gift, yet I also believe that it is a gift that, even if modestly bestowed, can be cultivated. The cultivation of humor is a matter of constant attentiveness to the incongruities between God's will and our own, God's intent for Creation and the world's will for itself. Scripture is a great help. I recommend frequent forays into the Gospel of John. There, the people around Jesus, the beneficiaries of his instruction, hardly ever get the point. Corpses are raised from the dead and water turns to wine just by his presence. Hardly anyone is able to get a handle on Jesus, so to speak, just like Mary Magdalene tried literally to do at Easter (John 20:17). When some doubt that he has been resurrected, Jesus responds by asking them if they have any fish for breakfast (21:5).

⎯⎯⎯ ⎯⎯⎯ ⎯⎯⎯ ⎯⎯⎯ ⎯⎯⎯

Because we preachers must, at least on a yearly basis, preach resurrection, we keep being challenged to minister in the light of the resurrection. We are not permitted the old excuse for lethargy, "people don't change." Certainly, everything we know about people suggests that they usually don't change. But sometimes they do. Change is rare; indeed it would be considered virtually impossible were it not that Jesus has been raised from the dead. When a pastor keeps working with some suffering parishioner even when there is no discernible change in that person's life or when a pastor keeps preaching the truth even with no visible congregational response, that pastor is being a faithful witness to the resurrection (Luke 1:2). That preacher is continuing to be obedient to the charge of the angel at the tomb to go and tell something that has changed the fate of the world (Matt. 28:7).

I love that incident in Luke when, after Jesus has sent out the Seventy to preach, to heal, and to proclaim peace—in short, to do the same ministry that he himself has been doing—the Seventy "return with joy" (Luke 10:17). It works! We are actually ministers! "In your name even the demons submit to us!"

Jesus breaks into their report with, "I watched Satan fall from heaven like a flash of lightning" (10:18). In other words, this ministry is much more than helping people, more even than healing or preaching. Something grand, sweeping, and cosmic is being worked out through us and our work. This is bigger than we imagined. God is taking back the whole cosmos through our faithful work. We are not only fulfilling the task assigned to us by the bishop, our "names are written in heaven" (10:20). What we tend to think of as the humdrum tasks of ministry are in reality a kind of cosmic war: "For our struggle is not against enemies of blood and flesh, but against the rulers, against the authorities, against the cosmic powers of this present darkness, against the spiritual forces of evil in the heavenly places." (Eph. 6:12)

There is thus something inherent in the practice of ministry that keeps Christian ministry predisposed toward expectation of miracle, surprise, and change. Easter ought to make us more persistent, more willing to engage in recklessness derived from our anticipation of the future. Lacking the empowerment provided by the resurrection, we are always in danger of falling back upon common sense, what is "realistic" or "responsible." Easter people ought to be more foolish than that.